Narrative Generation

*Why narrative will become your most
valuable asset in the next 5 years*

Ann **Badillo**
Tim **Donovan**
Tobin **Trevarthen**

21st Century Narrative
http://www.narrativegeneration.com/

Narrative Generation: a book/by Ann Badillo, Tim Donovan, Tobin Trevarthen

Layout design by Ross Burck - rossburck@gmail.com

Published in the United States of America

Table of Contents

AUTHORS

Principal Authors

Ann Badillo, Tim Donovan, Tobin Trevarthen

Modeling + Writing

Joe Sterling

Editor

Dorothy Pomerantz

MANY THANKS TO THE "BOOK SWARM"

Design + Facilitation

Joe Sterling

Graphics & Glyphs

Alicia Bramlett

Crew

Meg Buzzi
Tess Christy
Neder Gatmon-Segal
Beth Marx
Fedor Ovchinnikov
Dana Pearlman

Mia Pond
Sonia Sawhney
Olivia Trevarthen
Tatyana Vekovishcheva
Taylor Wilkins

Participants

Remi Adams
Giannella Alvarez
Grace Angulo
Lisa Atwood
Corinne Augustine
Jeanine Becker
Alex Black
DeeAnn Bundey
Peter Coughlan
Mike Courtney
Shaun Daniels
Zac Fisher
Whitney Greer
Lisa Gerould
Ron Glotzer
Julee Hermann
Jayne Hillman
Tirza Hollenhorst
Roman Honeycutt
Andrew Juncker
Jeff Kell

Kathia Laszlo
Matt Levine
James Park
Mike Parsons
Kathleen Paylor
Martin Pidel
Jim Pisz
Tony Pribyl
Dana Masuda
Maureen McCarthy
Zelle Nelson
Heather Regan
Carol Rooney
Rafa Saavedra
Leon Segal
Whitney Smith
Barbara Tien
Roger Tsai
Ibanga Umanah
Amy Williams
Brandt Williams

At a time when we've all become obsessed
with the power of storytelling, I've become
increasingly focused on the missed opportunity
to harness the much greater power of narratives,
especially for institutions. In a time of mounting
performance pressure and growing uncertainty,
narratives will make the difference. — John Hagel

FOREWORD

THE NOISE HAS REACHED an almost deafening level. Voices, stories, competing messages and the pace of the 24/7 news cycle claw away at us. Taken individually, these stories have little or no meaning. There is no context.

We navigate and filter the noise as best we can — but technology and the always-on media saturate nearly every moment of our lives. (Even those of us in PR and journalism — whose job it is to filter the noise — start to feel panicky.) We struggle to map, prioritize and make sense of the stories that surround us. These stories directly influence our personal, community and global perspectives. How can the meaningful information, which can help guide our decision-making and influence our belief systems, get through? How can we collect and then translate stories into something more meaningful?

There is a tool that we can use to help bring order to all of this informational chaos: narrative. It organizes stories, adds order, provides context, helps to inform our belief systems and motivates us to respond.

Narrative is a framework designed to help individuals and organizations cut through the noise and reach the people whom they most want to align with, influence or activate. But the act of building narrative has, until now, been something of a mystery. What differentiates narrative from story? How do you write your organization's narrative? How do you know if the narrative you're creating is strong?

Those of us exploring the impact of narrative in the 21st century believe that there needs to be a new model for building creative and powerful narratives.

With the intention of building that model, 50 executives with backgrounds in business, technology, education, filmmaking, religious studies, product development, branding and advertising gathered in an unfinished storefront in Oakland on a muggy day in July for a book swarm — an ambitious but truly exciting event to co-create this book in one day. Arriving in the morning to a pop-up design space located next to Oakland's famous entrepreneurial co-working center the Impact Hub Oakland, none of the participants were sure how, or if, the process was going to work.

This book and model are the result of that day. The book swarm kicked off The Narrative Project, a movement to help individuals, entrepreneurs, companies, social organizers and other influencers to effectively understand, define and then build their own narratives.

A spirit of collaboration infused the event and by the end of the day, we had collectively reached a consensus about what narrative means and how we can use this new model to create powerful narratives in the 21st century. All we had to work with that day were giant whiteboards, coffee and a lot of brainpower. But in the hands of seasoned event designers and facilitators, those 50 people produced an amazing example of group genius. Each person brought his or her own experience and understanding of narrative to the process. Together, we were able to rapidly prototype a narrative model that otherwise would have taken years to produce. The model presented in this book takes its cue from the work done during the book swarm.

So what do we mean when we talk about narrative? In this book you will learn what narrative is and why it is important. You will learn the conditions that give rise to a narrative. You will get a sense of the basic roles of the participants in the dance of narrative. We call them narrative "Initiators" and "Respondents." You will also learn about the elements of the existing narratives you live with, and are yourself creating.

There are many ways in which we all experience narratives. They help us make sense of our own ideas and the world around us. Narratives help us to define our individual belief systems and inspire us to take action. Narratives give us a frame for understanding, organizing and contextualizing stories in a way that brings both order and much-needed clarity to the chaos of modern life.

Narrative is relatable. By touching something universal in us, narrative brings us together to better understand the world and ourselves.

Narrative is contextual. It reflects the here and now and helps us define who we are (or are not) in relation to our peers and in relation to our past, present and potential future.

Narrative is inspirational. An important effect of narrative is that it invites and inspires the listener, or "Respondent," to actively engage in it and to participate. In the best cases, that engagement can impact the Respondent's outlook on life. Ideally, it inspires us to become a narrator who then extends, modifies and perpetuates the narrative. Narratives behave like living ecologies and exert a force on the communities in which they move and evolve. Narratives are how we consciously or unconsciously craft our perceptions.

Narratives are also transcendent, in that the meaning and purpose of narrative is vastly relatable regardless of age, race, faith, gender, orientation, etc. A true narrative connects many who resonate with the narrative's theme.

This book will help you:

- Understand what a narrative is and the dynamic conditions from which it emerges
- Recognize both the authentic (and false) narratives that surround and impact you
- Become more conscious of the narratives in your life, organization and community so you can exert choice to align with or modify the narratives around you
- Appreciate the fundamental roles people play in creating and responding to narratives
- Understand the building blocks that make up a narrative
- Create new narratives for personal, business or community improvement

The working metaphor for narrative that emerged during the book swarm was that of a mosaic. These artworks have been around for centuries. They can be found around the world in many countries and in many cultures. Mosaics are made up of thousands of small pieces of glass, pottery or stone called tesserae. Seen separately, the tesserae don't look like much. But put together, they create a work of art. Mosaics combine the old (broken shards) with the new (mortar) to build a new whole that blends the past and the now. Mosaics have been telling visual stories for centuries in churches, synagogues and other places of worship around the globe.

Like mosaics, narratives are informed by the past but firmly rooted in the present. In narrative, stories are the tessera pieces that, when joined together, create form and sustain the narrative.

Since narratives are dynamic, evolving ecologies of related, contextual stories, we will think of narrative as a "living mosaic." We'll use this analogy to help you grasp our new model for narrative analysis and creation.

Our intent is that this book will be provocative, practical and inspiring for people trying to build narratives. It is our sincere hope that you will use our model to create powerful new narratives that will improve your personal and professional lives.

About Narrative Pattern Language

Throughout this book you will find glyphs, small symbols that represent different narratives. Inspired by Christopher Alexander's architectural pattern language, these glyphs are meant to help you visualize the narratives that surround you and think visually about the narratives this book will help you create. We invite you to share new glyphs that represent your unique narratives at: www.narrativegeneration.com

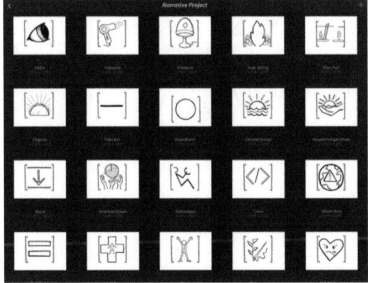

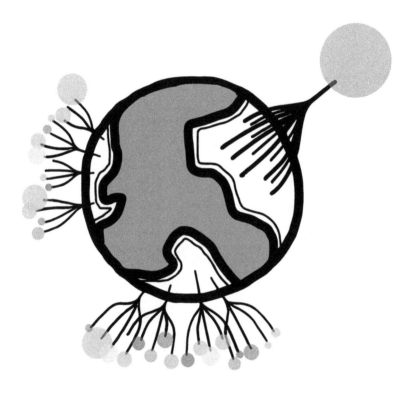

CHAPTER I

INTRODUCTION — WHAT IS NARRATIVE?

A LITTLE GIRL IN a red cape leaves her safe home for the dangerous woods. Carrying a basket of food for her ill grandmother, she becomes an object of desire for a hungry wolf with bad intentions.

A beautiful princess is marked for death by her evil stepmother. She hides in the woods but the queen still finds her and poisons her with a bright red apple.

Facing starvation, a father gives in to his wife's demands to leave their two children in the woods. Hungry and lost, the children stumble upon a house built of candy. When they take a bite, the witch inside traps them for her own meal.

We all know these stories. Our parents read them to us when we were children, and for many of us, tales like Red Riding Hood, Snow White and Hansel and Gretel helped build a foundation for the adults we would become.

These Grimms' fairy tales tell different stories, yet they echo the same narrative: "The world is a dangerous place." The woods always represent the wider, scary world. Children need to know that in the woods, wolves will try to eat them; if a kindly old woman offers shiny red apples, she may not have the best of intentions; and houses made out of candy are better left alone. Parents hope that if their children can learn even a small amount of caution from these fanciful tales, they'll be safer and more aware of the perils around them when they leave home.

These stories have survived over time not just because they are terrific tales but because of the narrative that links them. "The world is a dangerous place" is a universally relatable lesson with no beginning and no end. It has evolved over time as the dangers facing children have changed. Different communities and different cultures can tell their own stories around this narrative to make it more relatable. The narrative reflects a shared value and gives us a way to talk about something difficult. And there is a call to action inherent in the narrative. Children must change their ways, become more aware and walk more cautiously through the world as they grow older.

Fairy tales like these may seem simple, but they illustrate a complicated point: Narrative is not a story. Too often people use those terms interchangeably, but they are not the same. Narrative is the glue that connects stories and gives them context and meaning. Stories are the tales that exist within a narrative. To continue our living mosaic theme — stories are the tesserae that form the living mosaic. The narrative provides the contextual framework and the mortar that connects all the pieces. When the stories and other elements of the narrative are brought together, they can exert a force on society and create change.

The difference between story and narrative is a crucial element of the teachings of John Hagel, founder of the Deloitte Center for the Edge and the godfather of defining narrative for the 21st century. Mr. Hagel has been evangelizing narrative for businesses since about 2011. He sees narrative as a great differentiator that can "help a company stand out from the crowd in a powerful and sustainable way."[i]

Hagel points to two crucial differences between story and narrative. Stories are self-contained; they have an arc that includes a beginning, middle and end. Narratives are open-ended. Red Riding Hood left for Grandma's house. Along the way she met a wolf who wanted to eat her. The wolf pretended to be her grandmother and ate her. A woodsman came and rescued her, end of story.

But there is no true beginning or end to the idea that the world is a dangerous place. The narrative connects the audience to a persistent theme that they can own and incorporate into their everyday lives. The aspirational element (be safer in the world) gives the audience something to strive for.

Another difference between stories and narrative: Stories are about the storyteller or specific characters and moments in time. Narratives, on the other hand, are thematic streams of consciousness. The impact of the narrative depends greatly on how actively the listener or Respondent engages or interacts. To quote Hagel again: "The resolution of narrative depends on the choice you make and the action you take — you will determine the outcome." Hagel clarifies this by saying, "And the resolution of that narrative hinges on you — it hinges on the choices and actions you are going to take. ... So narrative is key in terms of inspiration and focus and movement to action."[ii] In short, the impact of narrative on anyone is completely dependent on the way they either choose to participate in the narrative ... or not.

Look at the narrative of marriage equality as an example. "Everyone should be allowed to marry whomever they love" is a narrative that has gained an enormous amount of traction over the last decade because of the way listeners have engaged with it. The narrative speaks to a universal need (love) and has moved people to take action, whether that meant marching for equality, sending a letter to a congressman or sharing #lovewins on social media platforms like Instagram and Twitter. That active involvement fed the narrative and made it even more powerful. Ultimately, it helped created a significant change in our government policies toward marriage of same-sex couples.

Narratives like the one inherent in fairy tales move us away from danger while narratives like marriage equality might move us to help others. In this way, narrative can be powerfully generative. Regardless of the direction of a narrative, what are its most basic elements?

Narrative, in simplest terms, comprises the interplay between three components: **context, drive** and **meaning**. These three components describe the conditions needed to give rise to a narrative.

Context: How does a narrative relate to its moment in history and the communities initiating and responding to it?

Drive: What is the intent of those initiating the narrative and what impact is it having on Respondents?

Meaning: How does the narrative change current assumptions and inspire new beliefs?

<u>Why narrative?</u>

Narrative isn't just for children and delivering cautionary tales. More and more, people, organizations and businesses are searching for narratives to help them understand and explain themselves and the world around them. We have become a society overwhelmed by stories. Social media sites, round-the-clock news, thousands of TV channels and millions of websites, blogs and social feeds vie for our attention with story after story. We are deafened by the noise. The effect is exhausting and overwhelming. Without a perceptual framework to filter meaning from the noise, all that media is just meaningless static. As Nobel laureate and social scientist Herbert A. Simon said, "A wealth of information creates a poverty of attention." And without attention, there can be no understanding.

Narrative is a framework of meaning that helps us focus our attention, make sense and build understanding. Our personal narrative is the framework that bridges what we hold dear inside and what is happening in the world. Our narrative framework makes it possible to perceive what is important to us and to our community by putting our values into stark relief against the background noise. Narrative brings our chosen "big picture" into focus.

In Chapters 2 and 3 we lay out the problems we face as a society and how the problems can be fixed using narrative. Chapter 4 looks at who are Initiators and who are Respondents. Chapter 5 explains what makes a narrative authentic and Chapter 6 breaks down the anatomy of a narrative.

In Chapter 7 you will learn how to analyze the narratives that

impact your world and how to build new narratives for yourself
or your organization. Building a narrative requires asking some
penetrating questions. We've laid out those questions in Chapter 7,
which you can use as a workbook.

<u>Our definition</u>
Our group was inspired by Hagel but wanted to find practical
ways to apply his ideas. Here is a breakdown of how we define
narrative.
What is a narrative?
A narrative is a thematic ecology of related, contextual stories
that inform and define one's perspective.
How do narratives come into being?
Narratives emerge as a force among participants crafting
perspective over time.
How do narratives behave?
A narrative behaves like a living mosaic of interconnected
stories and themes.
How do we get value from narratives?
Narratives inform and define one's perspective.
What is the most important element of a narrative?
It is crucial that narrative be authentic.
Who cares?
Your audience comprises all the Respondents to your narrative:
the passive, the reactive and those with intentions of their own.

<u>Who needs narrative?</u>
If you're reading this book, you already sense that you need
to be better at analyzing and creating narrative. You likely fall
into one of four categories. As a reminder, when we use the term
"organization" throughout this book, that entity could be a business,

a nonprofit, a social movement or a large institution.

Independent Business People

With the rise of the sharing economy and the demise of old corporate structures, more people than ever are working for themselves. The lack of job security can be terrifying but it can also be an opportunity. Entrepreneurial contract workers need to set themselves apart from the crowd and the best way to do that is through the use of a personal narrative. A narrative can also help connect you with similarly minded people in your field. It gives you a way to open a door for networking and business opportunities. Personal narrative may be the story of your life but the narrative of your independent business should be one that is persistent, flexible and contains a call to action. Oprah Winfrey is a great exemplar of an individual businessperson who has cultivated a strong narrative — "Anyone can help themselves." This defines everything she does, every story she tells and every business she invests in. An empire has formed around Oprah and that narrative. Not everyone can be Oprah, but that doesn't mean you shouldn't strive to create your own powerful narrative.

Large Organization Trying to Change

Businesses, nonprofits and government organizations get stuck in all sorts of ruts: sales decline, competition in a crowded field creates more hurdles to success or the organization may simply need to overhaul its mission or brand because it has lost meaning and relevance in its marketing. Whatever the reason for the change, narrative can help.

In 2014, the drugstore chain CVS rebranded itself CVS Health. True to its new narrative of putting customer health first, CVS took the dramatic step of ending cigarette sales. Continuing to sell cigarettes would make CVS' new brand unauthentic. At the time, the company estimated it would lose $2 billion in revenue in the first year by dropping tobacco sales. But the move helped boost CVS' stock price. Almost a year after ending cigarette sales, CVS' stock price was up 50 percent per share and revenues were actually up, not down.[iii] Its new narrative not only became more authentic, but CVS became more aligned with the general trend in the market toward wellness. Interestingly, Rite Aid has followed suit by redesigning store interiors to emphasize wellness.

Social Causes and Impact Organizations

It is almost impossible to inspire people to take a stand on a social issue without a strong narrative. The things that make a good narrative are: addressing a common point of pain or "resistance," a transcendent context, a strong contrast between the new values and the background status quo, and a call to action. These are the same things that social causes need to define themselves and to influence people.

Social movements are born out of civil, cultural, ethnic, religious, gender or political friction, and friction is also what gives rise to the best narratives. A strong authentic narrative can unite several organizations under one umbrella and galvanize people to change the world.

Black Lives Matter is a perfect example of a social cause built around a successful narrative. Formed after the murder of Trayvon Martin, Black Lives Matter helped connect what once would have been seen as disparate stories about black people being killed. By pulling these stories together into one ongoing narrative and inspiring people to talk about the killings on social media, Black Lives Matter helped change the national dialogue around race in America. Out of the ashes of terrible events, narratives can become a powerful center of gravity to rally communities.

Brands

It's no longer enough for a brand manager to focus simply on the brand's story. Stories are static and centrally controlled. Central control in the age of social media is a nostalgic illusion. All brands have a narrative but they likely don't know what it is. What brands need is a deliberately initiated and maintained narrative. Narratives inspire connection and action among customers and other stakeholders. Narratives exist across many types of media. Brands used to focus on TV, print and banner ads. It was good enough to present a quick anecdote. But today, brands need to generate loyal long-term followers in places like Twitter, Instagram, Snapchat and Facebook. That requires dialogue and relationships. Stories are a one-way message — a monologue, if you will — while narratives are an interactive dialogue or conversation. All brands are living a narrative, most by accident. Only when a brand authentically lives an intentional narrative will it build real social currency with its audience.

Red Bull has one of the strongest brand narratives around. The narrative of living an adventurous, energetic life permeates everything the company does. Through its narrative, Red Bull has become synonymous with an extreme sports lifestyle. And you don't have to be an extreme athlete to take part in the narrative. It appeals to Respondents who are bungee-jumping off of bridges or just trying to find the energy to get through an all-nighter. When the energy drink sponsored Felix Baumgartner's jump from space, no one questioned what a caffeine drink had to do with space. Red Bull's Respondents got the connection immediately (extreme to the max) and the stunt felt perfectly aligned with Red Bull's narrative.

Narrative: a living mosaic

With that overview of what narrative is and who needs it, let's explore a deeper way to think about narrative. By the end of this book, you'll have a solid understanding of the anatomy of narrative and you'll be introduced to tools you can use to analyze your current narrative and build your own intentional narrative. But first, here's a useful way to think about narrative — as a living mosaic.

When building mosaics, tesserae (the pieces that make up a mosaic) can come from anywhere. They can be found in nature (like stones, pebbles or even plants), they can come from the past (shards of old pottery or mature trees) or they can be newly crafted (glass or plants from seed). Looking at a collection of random tesserae, you could not predict the finished mosaic. But when each piece is arranged in the artist's context (her era, geography and community), according to her big-picture design (intention), her mosaic emerges as a new artistic whole (with new meaning) against the background where it is installed (the current meaning). What her audience says about the mosaic and how they interact with it determines the mosaic's value (the narrative's impact).

We recommend that you approach this book with an open mind. When you begin to analyze your current narrative, look into it deeply, vulnerably and honestly. You will be able to take what you find and craft a new narrative that resonates with your audience and has staying power.

Things to think about:

- How do you define narrative? What analogies help you describe it?
- As an individual, what is a narrative from your upbringing that frames your life?
- How could you benefit from an updated personal narrative of your own crafting?
- What is the narrative that frames your organization?
- How could your organization benefit from an updated and intentional narrative?
- What values do you want to come through in your personal narrative?
- How would you contrast your organization's current narrative (background) with a new narrative (foreground)? Would there be resistance to the new narrative?

	Community	Context
CONTEXT	**Community** • Narrators/Filters • Story Tellers • Audiences	**Context** • Era/Time Horizon • Rate of Change • Geographies/Networks
MEANING	**Current Meaning** Narrative in **Background:** • Current Assumptions • Current Belief System • Current Aspirations • Current Linguistic Frames	**New Meaning** New **Contrasting** Narrative: • New Assumptions • New Belief Ssstem • New Aspirations • New Linguistic Frames
DRIVE	**Intent of Initiator** • Values • Misison & Vision • Strategic Themes • Intended Layering	**Impact in Respondents** • Changes Made • Actions Taken • Value Created • Other Evidence

CHAPTER 2

TOO MANY STORIES, NOT ENOUGH NARRATIVE

IN TODAY'S WORLD, WE are more connected than ever before. That can be a good thing. Families divided by thousands of miles can share photos and video-chat to stay in touch. We can access almost any music or movie we want at any time. And the incredible quantity of information available on the Internet makes it possible to research any topic we can imagine, from space travel to the thickness of a butterfly's wing.

But connection comes at a price when we are constantly bombarded by information. According to Nielsen Media Research, the average adult spends over 11 hours per day on some kind of device. Considering people are only awake about 16 hours per day, that means that many of those hours are likely spent looking at more than one device.[iv]

The vast majority of that "device time" (4 hours and 51

minutes) is spent watching TV, but the amount of time we spend on our computers and cell phones is climbing. In 2012 computers and phones occupied roughly two hours of each day. Today, we spend an average 2.5 hours per day on the Internet and our phones. According to a Gallup Poll, 41 percent of adults check their cell phones several times an hour, and 11 percent say they check their phones every few minutes.[v]

For the most part, we are consuming and digesting stories. TV provides us with an endless array of stories — from high-quality, challenging shows like "Mad Men" to the escapist pleasures of "The Real Housewives of New York." There are 30-second stories in ads. News stations assail us with breaking news alerts (it seems like even the smallest development now qualifies as breaking news). Sports coverage has become an endless parade of triumph-of-the-human-spirit stories and gladiator contests with David vs. Goliath odds.

On social networks we share thousands of little stories about our own lives. A friend posts photos from a rafting trip; another shares a news article about the drought in California. On Twitter, stories fly by so quickly it's almost impossible not to miss something. A story about sharks might be followed by a tweet about the economy followed by a review of the latest movie to hit theaters.

News sites compete for our attention with increasingly sensational headlines and "clickbait." If you've ever clicked on a link because the headline said something like "You won't believe what she did next ...," then you know these kinds of articles. Despite our best intentions, we are sucked into the drama and find ourselves clicking on meaningless stories again and again.

All of this clicking takes a real toll on our brains. Daniel J. Levitin, the author of "The Organized Mind: Thinking Straight in the Age of Information Overload," calls all of our checking of

Facebook, Twitter, texts and email a "neural addiction." He says that every time we check a feed we (falsely) feel a little more connected socially and we experience something novel. That doles out a little more reward hormone in our brain.[vi]

But it rewards the pleasure-seeking region of our brain, not the "higher-level thought centers in the prefrontal cortex." The information overload becomes like alcohol, fun at first and then very hard to give up.

"A wealth of information creates a poverty of attention."

As our attention spans shrink, even the idea of reading an entire article becomes too much. Give us the information in a 140-character tweet or a GIF story or we won't stay interested. To paraphrase the great media critic Marshall McLuhan, the medium becomes the message. And today, the message is increasingly hard to understand.

The experience is like looking at random jigsaw puzzle pieces thrown on the floor. We don't see any connection and while individual pieces might stand out, we can't form them into any kind of a complete image.

What is missing is a unifying narrative. When we apply a narrative to the morass of information, we can connect some of the pieces and see a coherent image. As those pieces come together and are contrasted against the background of confusion, meaning pops into view. If it is clear enough, we can communicate that meaning to others and take action.

Unlike the quick-hit pleasure of social media, narrative nourishes our brains. We know a new narrative is taking hold when we feel compelled to speak out and share a set of messages about it. Some narratives are so strong that they change our entire view of the world and make us question ideas we previously considered fact. There was a time when the prevailing narrative described the world as flat. There was a time when the prevailing narrative held that human activity could not influence the climate. In both cases the new narratives provoked radical transformations in human civilization. Narratives are a force to be reckoned with.

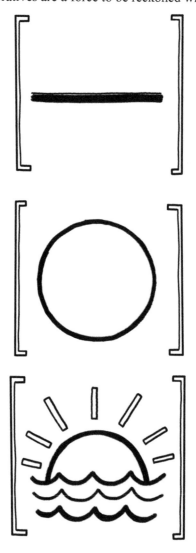

A word about story

Although we want to make clear the distinction between story and narrative, we need to take a moment to talk about story. Stories are the engines that activate narratives. The narrative Initiator is counting on the Respondents to become participants in their own right who will perpetuate the narrative.

Those stories can have a very powerful effect on our brains. According to researchers in Spain, stories not only activate the expected parts of our brains (language processing, etc.) but also light up the regions of our brains that would be active if we were experiencing the events in the story.

Not only that, but the brains of the people telling and listening to the story can synchronize, according to Uri Hasson, an associate professor of psychology at Princeton University. By telling a story, you can plant ideas, emotions and inspiration in your listener's brain. That's a very powerful thing. And when the stories are connected in a narrative, that power grows exponentially.[vii]

Let's go back to the example of Oprah. Her narrative ("Anyone can help themselves") is so clear and so consistent that if you only read Oprah-approved media and watched Oprah-approved shows, her narrative would be the one thought connecting everything in your world. You might start your day with a relaxing Oprah chai tea latte at Starbucks. In the morning you could read O, The Oprah Magazine to get tips on healthy cooking and kitchen designs you could do yourself. Later in the afternoon you might watch Oprah protégé Dr. Oz talk about the advantages of avoiding caffeine. All of the stories in your world would align into a beautiful, contextual whole. You might even find yourself reciting an Oprah-like mantra: "I *can* help myself."

Things to think about:

- How do you experience the overwhelming number of stories thrown at you each day?
- What are some ways you can cut through the clutter?
- What are some examples of narratives that come through clearly over and over that relate to you and your belief systems?
- Is there "one thought" that seems to connect the dots for you — your narrative?

CHAPTER 3

THE NEW JOURNALISM, EVERYONE'S A STORYTELLER

ACCREDITED, PROFESSIONAL JOURNALISM IS becoming increasingly irrelevant. Take someone like Nate Silver as an example. A statistician by trade (and diehard baseball fan), Silver, on his own time, built PECOTA, the Player Empirical Comparison and Optimization Test Algorithm. PECOTA projects baseball players' performance based on historical information. It was an instant hit with sports fans. Silver then put his statistician's mind to the presidential election in 2008; he correctly predicted the election's outcome in 49 out of 50 states.

Nate Silver is now one of the most influential voices in politics and sports. His FiveThirtyEight blog ran on the New York Times website for three years and today draws plenty of eyeballs to ESPN. com. Silver works within the journalism establishment, but he's emblematic of the changing face of storytelling.

The publications that once acted as trusted gatekeepers to information, like The New York Times, Time magazine and even USA Today, are laying off hundreds of staff writers in favor of people like Silver — individual brands that bring a following with them. (Silver has since left the Times and now runs his own blog through ESPN.) At the same time, places like Fox News are famous for narrowing their content to select brands and individuals that produce a pervasive, and more or less aligned, narrative.

Today, whether you realize it or not, you are a storyteller. So is your Aunt Sally, your crazy neighbor and everyone you work with. We used to rely on journalists to be the gatekeepers — elevating the stories we needed to know and discarding the junk — and we trusted them to filter for verifiable facts. Today, we are all journalists and we all have access to the same technology as Nate Silver.

What's more, the corporate media streams we once trusted now present "infotainment" that has (in the famous words of Stephen Colbert) "truthiness" but not necessarily verifiable facts. The importance of old-school gatekeepers like The New York Times and Newsweek magazine is fading. According to a survey by the Pew Research Center, a majority of Facebook and Twitter users get their news from social networks. In 2013, 47 percent of users said they get their news from Facebook and 52 percent said they get their news from Twitter. In 2015 numbers for both sites were up to 63 percent.[viii]

As individual posters to blogs or social media services, we are not journalists in the traditional sense. We did not attend journalism school or put in our 10,000 hours. But we do tell stories and we choose which stories we want to share.

Getting, liking and sharing news on social media sites turns us all into gatekeepers. Whether we are the Initiator of the news or responding to it, we are each our own little Huffington Post, aggregating news from our trusted sources on the topics that get our attention. It can feel quite powerful to curate the stories into your own news feed (and sites like Paper.li explicitly let you build and share your own publications). But this new reality creates problems beyond the loss of critical insight and journalistic integrity.

The filter bubble

Internet activist Eli Pariser of MoveOn.org coined the term "filter bubble" in 2011. He used it to talk about the way search engines cater to each person differently. For example, someone who searches for the word "election" in 2016 might get served up websites linking to candidates Hillary Clinton or Bernie Sanders if that person was tagged as a progressive by her search history. Someone tagged as a conservative might get Donald Trump or Jeb Bush websites and a movie fan might get links about the 1999 movie Election.

Through social media, we also create our own filter bubbles. We tend to follow and like people who share our personal narrative — we tend to like people whose values, vision and perspectives match our own. A middle-aged baseball fan who is obsessed with his diet but loves craft beer will (purposefully or not) tailor his feed to match his tastes. Sites like Facebook also use algorithms in an attempt to make your feed more relevant. The more baseball stories our sports fan clicks on, the more baseball stories he's going to get. A story on, say, breastfeeding might not ever make it to the top of his feed — that is, until his new child is born and he starts reading more about pregnancy and childbirth.

These filter bubbles artificially skew our view of reality. We get stuck in reinforcing feedback loops. We inadvertently increase our exposure to stories that align with our belief systems. We turn down stories that make us uncomfortable because they challenge our current narrative, and then our online information source amplifies this effect with news-aggregating algorithms. By limiting what we hear and see, we limit our ability to see the other side. It's easy enough to find a different opinion. But filters make us lazy. It's so much easier to just read our own personalized news, which reflects our personalized narrative, than to look deeper into any issues. This can make us incredibly narrow-minded.

Filter bubbles also deplete empathy. We may have lots of common experiences with people who share our exact mindset, but we have fewer experiences with people outside of our immediate circle. When we don't see a wide spectrum of humanity (with all of its flaws and in all its glory), we lose empathy for people whose experiences are very different from ours. We too often see people with other viewpoints as belonging to uniform groups that think and act the same — we label their narrative as if it were their actual identity: He's a tree hugger; she's a conservative; he's a jock; she's a soccer mom. It's hard to have compassion for a faceless population whose narrative runs counter to our own. At the same time, it is hard to see the flaws in narratives we feel strongly aligned with.

While a new narrative can connect stories and create a call to action, our familiar filter bubble allows us to sit back and do nothing, safe in our nonthreatening recycled news feed. Our filters ensure that our incoming information proves us right. Our perception is reinforced that the world is aligned with our background narrative. This makes it very hard for new narratives to motivate us even when they would improve our health, relationships, prosperity, local environment and community life.

A filter bubble might feel like a narrative but it's not. It is rather the effect of a narrative in action. A narrative may cause your personal scope to narrow, but that is not the same thing as creating a true narrative. Narratives are carefully constructed. Filter bubbles arise almost accidentally, because the narratives we live by generally go unexamined while the filters continue to run in the background. Most people wouldn't say they want to see the world through one small peephole, but that is effectively how many now experience reality.

The death of truth

When news flies by at 140 characters per second, truth takes a backseat to speed. This isn't a new phenomenon. Journalists have always placed a premium on "scoops." But as more and more people try to be first with the story, the whole truth has become less important.

The speed at which news travels around the Internet can be incredibly dangerous for anyone who cares about truth. Two days after the Boston Marathon bombing, several news outlets reported that the FBI had made an arrest in the case, saying the suspect was a "dark-skinned male."[ix] In reality no arrest had been made, and the FBI warned that the false reports endangered their investigation. When an arrest was finally made, it turned out that the suspects were Chechen brothers. (One brother was killed in a police shootout, the other was convicted.) The initial news not only put the investigation at risk but also played into racist perceptions about criminals.

Many untruths floating around on the Internet are subtler. Wikipedia entries change at the drop of a hat and while they shouldn't be taken for truth, they too often are. Biased media outlets report news through their own lenses, failing to give it context. That kind of reporting can often make a story look like the truth when it is really just one side of the story. As news outlets rush to get the news out too quickly and pick and choose what they report to fit their own bias, readers start to mistrust sources that were once seen as the establishment.

Perceptions are treated as reality. When what we take on board is a lie or even just a simple error, the damage can last for years after the story has faded. Lindsey Stone, a caregiver for adults with learning disabilities, lost her job after a photo of her pretending to shout and giving the middle finger at Arlington National Cemetery made the rounds in 2012. Taken out of context, the photo seemed incredibly disrespectful. But, as documented by Jon Ronson in his book "So You've Been Publicly Shamed," the photo was part of an inside joke between Stone and her friend, who always took pictures of themselves doing silly stunts, like smoking in front of no-smoking signs. Somehow, a private photo meant to be between a few friends (who would see it in context) went public and Stone was vilified and turned into a pariah.[x]

Again, this story might be mistaken for narrative but it is not. The story of Lindsey Stone as someone who disrespected veterans was completely inauthentic. It was inaccurate and devoid of context. The story was syndicated and shared by thousands of people who thought they were seeing the whole picture and happily contributed to Stone's takedown.

A reputation may take years to build, but can be decimated in weeks.

The easy dissemination of false information has made us all inherently distrustful. We desperately seek out voices we trust and cling to them like life preservers. The growing cynicism gives outsized power to people whom we do trust (even though their "truth" might just be echoing what we want to hear, not objective truth). This makes it that much harder for new voices to prove their credibility and to be heard.

The layering effect

In new media and online, a story doesn't end once the final word is written. Thanks to comments, reshares and aggregation, stories grow, morph and change once they are out in the ether. These layers are like new plants being added to a formal garden. A formal garden can become more exquisite or turn into a jungle depending on how plantings are layered and tended. The same is true for narratives.

A good example of this layering effect is the resignation of Ellen Pao, the former CEO at Reddit. The online forum prides itself on openness and freedom of speech (to the point of allowing people to say some incredibly sexist and racist things). But when a popular employee was fired, the community fought back, shutting down forums in protest. CEO Pao tried to make things right with the community but eventually stepped down from her post. Because Pao had previously fought a gender discrimination suit against her then employer Kleiner Perkins Caufield & Byers, many jumped to the conclusion that Pao had been fired simply for being a woman. (Speed is the death of truth.) The story quickly morphed into one about the very real problem of the way women are treated in Silicon Valley.

But it turns out sexism likely didn't play a role in Pao leaving Reddit. A New York Times story about Pao carried the headline "It's Silicon Valley 2, Ellen Pao 0: Fighter of Sexism Is Out at Reddit." The newspaper's public editor, Margaret Sullivan, took the writers to task for framing the story around sexism instead of Pao's problems at Reddit, saying that the news story had verged into the realm of opinion.[xi]

What mattered here were the frames each individual storyteller put around the story. The frames influenced the layers being contributed to Pao's story. George Lakoff, a linguist and framer of political language, reminds us that "frames are mental structures that shape the way we see the world. As a result, they shape the goals we seek, the plans we make, the way we act. … To change our frames [and, we would assert, narratives] is to change all of this."[xii] We need to be aware of our frames when we analyze narrative.

The story around Pao felt like narrative, but it wasn't. The layering effect only helped to confuse things. With the layers of commentary applied, it appeared that the narrative here was one of Pao continually facing (and fighting) discrimination. But that would have been a false (and therefore inauthentic) narrative. People put the story pieces together haphazardly and the result was a complete mess.

If you want your narrative to remain coherent, each new additional mosaic piece layered onto your mosaic needs to amplify and build upon those that came before. Those that are layered on by others need to be countered or reframed to serve your intended narrative.

The new PR

The new journalism has made the map that people and organizations used to follow to get their messages out irrelevant. In the past, anyone who wanted their story told could go to a public relations firm, pay some money and get the story out as intended. PR people developed relationships with journalists who were hungry for stories, and they knew how to throw the right event and invite the right people to create buzz.

Today, things are much more complicated. According to PR Week, the PR industry's magazine about itself, "The current perfect storm of a lackluster economy and a 24-hour news cycle, where individuals are just as responsible for disseminating the news as reporters, is helping give birth to a new type of hybrid creative agency. Brands ... have moved away from traditional advertising campaigns and have begun to integrate new strategic visions, to help make their company stand out at a fraction of the cost."[xiii]

Finding a way to reach an audience is increasingly difficult, and the frustration can be felt in every corner of the media, business and social justice worlds. Journalists have little time to filter story pitches that may be authentic and interesting but may be all hype and buzz. Sorting fact from fiction (and the honorable from shysters) can be really tough. Audiences are becoming increasingly savvy about marketing pitches and they refuse to engage with silly, fake "content." Our inboxes are overflowing with requests for money and time from political campaigns and charities. Instead of an elegantly patterned mosaic, we are overwhelmed by random tesserae. It becomes nearly impossible to make meaning. When a narrative is missing, either our own or one we embrace from outside, we are adrift, untethered, looking for a place to land. This is deeply unsettling to the mind and spirit, which is why curating a personal narrative is so important to a good life. It is equally important for organizations that want to do good and do well.

Things to think about:

- Whom do you trust to tell you truthful stories?
- How do you gauge the credibility of your sources?
- What platforms do you use to gather information? Are you subjected to a biased stream of stories that filters out anything you'd disagree with?
- Are you conscious of your filter bubble? If so, how does it influence your view of the world? How do you stay open to contrasting points of view?
- Where do you post or publish your stories? Where do you express opinion (likes, shares, etc.)?
- Do you think of yourself as a journalist?
- How does the new journalism complicate your ability to understand the world around you?
- How are you building on your narrative mosaic?

CHAPTER 4

NARRATIVE INITIATORS AND RESPONDENTS

IN THE LAST DECADE, storytelling as a craft and as a set of tools for influence, building culture and simply conveying the news has gained fresh prominence. Storytelling methods are being applied to everything from advertising to organizational changes to social impact. The tools for telling and distributing stories are multiplying like brooms in Disney's "Fantasia." When anyone can be a storyteller (who is amplified by the Internet), everyone has a chance to be heard and there is a lot more noise. When there is no longer a standard map for how to get your message out, you can forge your own path.

In the old model, the company, government or brand was the anointed and sovereign storyteller. Those storytellers could publish or broadcast an isolated story with some emotional resonance and connect to an audience. It could move audiences to buy a product or join a cause. But as we've shown in the last two chapters, that model no longer works. The sovereign storyteller now has no more power than an individual with a social media following. And one story, even from an authority, will not galvanize a movement.

We assert that by shifting your focus from telling stories to crafting a narrative, your voice becomes more expansive, clearer and more easily heard. Narrative tools can help you sort context, conflict and meaning instead of fighting against them. These tools will help your narrative stand out against a background of clutter.

It is critical to understand the contrast between an existing background narrative and a fresh narrative. Without that contrast there is nothing to distinguish the new from the old. Contrast can take many forms, the most direct being the idea of resistance. This might feel counterintuitive, but it is crucial to a strong narrative. "Breathing air is good" might make biological sense, but without resistance, it is not a narrative. "Protect clean air so future generations can breathe" is a strong narrative because it takes a position and acknowledges the opposition — that some believe that the air is fine as is and that clean-air regulations hurt business. Having something to react against lends texture to a narrative and reinforces its call to action. No contrast, no call to action, no new narrative.

So who is it that proposes a new narrative? Who decides whether there is contrast with the background narrative? To keep this simple, we'll call out two types of participants in this dance: the narrative Initiator and the narrative Respondent. At times we, as individuals, are both Initiator and Respondent. But for the purposes of learning what narrative is and how it works, we'll make a somewhat forced distinction for now. We'll come back to the nuances of how we switch roles a little further on.

The narrative Initiator

If storytellers are a dime a dozen and all competing for the same eyes and ears, we need to find an organizing principle that helps us send out a coherent signal, one that is in contrast to all that noise. We need to elevate our role from storyteller to narrative Initiator. Yes, ultimately a narrative will connect a string of stories and those stories should each have validity, sincerity and connection. But without contrast the context, connections and intended new meaning never come to the foreground. If narrative components never become distinguishable from the background, the audience is once again left adrift; they have nothing to respond to and you have no Respondents. When a fresh narrative breaks onto the scene, it walks onto the busy street of media and commands a response. Now you've got Respondents, and they have a way to make sense of the morass of stories flowing by them.

Let's examine the difference between telling a story and initiating a narrative. This will shed light on what it means to be a narrative Initiator. A story is a one-way street where one voice, the storyteller, tells you the way it is. As in, "Here are the events that happened during Red Riding Hood's harrowing trip into the woods." A narrative, on the other hand, is a dialogue, which is started by the narrative Initiator. A narrative like "The world is a dangerous place" has room for many different stories within it and many different interpretations, and while it may have been crafted by a narrative Initiator, it has room for many voices. Those voices come from Respondents, i.e., active storytellers, relatively passive audience members and even counter narrative Initiators.

We can exchange stories and engage in a dialogue about how and why "The world is a dangerous place." The narrative becomes richer when dissenting voices offer counterarguments (for example, how much more safety can be found in today's world compared to the past). We can collaborate on novel ideas about protecting children. We can take the narrative further and build a Facebook page about different ways to talk to children about the larger world. There are endless ways to grow, stretch and morph the narrative. All this growing, stretching and morphing is the product of the Initiator and the Respondents engaging with the narrative, sending volleys of content across and around the common media landscape in which narrative lives.

The linguistic frame used to initiate a narrative is of great importance. Peter Senge, lead author of "The Fifth Discipline Fieldbook," drives home the point: "We participate more deeply than we imagine in shaping the world that we perceive."[xiv]

A story has an arc with a definitive ending, whereas a narrative is endless. The narrative Initiator's focus is not on the outcome. The Initiator may frame the big-picture dialogue and invite us in, but beyond that they can only refine and cultivate the narrative to the extent they have the resources to do so.

Returning to our mosaic analogy for a moment, stories are

generally set in mortar before they are told. There is no changing the story — it is what it is. However, once a narrative is launched, the Initiator and Respondents find themselves in a collaborative art project. Together they dip into various buckets of tesserae (different stories, facts and perceptions) and put the pieces into the narrative framework. Rather than mortar that sets hard as for stories, in a narrative mosaic the tesserae are set in sand. This way, over time, mosaic pieces can be moved, shifted or replaced altogether. Over time, a more and more rich and nuanced image emerges; a coherent narrative "big picture," a living mosaic, emerges and begins its life and evolution.

Ideally, at any point in the process the whole mosaic/narrative is understandable and approachable, and gets more so as each new element is added, moved or replaced. Every day you encounter narratives that are either in early, middle or late stages of their life spans. If they are strong, they make sense at any phase of development. However, if you enter a story in the middle, without the context of the beginning, you're lost. Stories begin and end, narratives live and evolve. Storytellers deliver stories, narrative Initiators cultivate a dialogue. Respondents receive stories. Respondents participate in narratives.

Now we come to a crucial difference between the Initiator of a narrative and the storyteller. The new Initiator has to be willing to relinquish control of the narrative. Story is tightly controlled and belongs to the storyteller. Narrative, on the other hand, has to live inside an ecosystem of many participants: the narrative Initiator, active Respondents and passive audience members. You'll know when your narrative has started to get its own legs when active Respondents begin using stories to amplify, modify or contest your narrative. This comes in many forms, but the social media examples are perhaps the simplest: They like it, share it and/or comment on it (favorably or not so much). From there, they will start telling stories that accentuate the contrast that distinguishes your narrative from the background narratives. In this respect, the narrative Initiator is giving up control of the narrative.

Your Respondents will deepen the contrast between the background meanings and the new meaning through their own storytelling, and they will report on how your narrative's call to action made them feel, and what they did as a result of it. You'll know your narrative is fully alive when the people around you begin living it. You will hear them reflect your narrative's assumptions, belief systems, aspirations and linguistic frames. Active Respondents will make changes in their own lives based on your narrative and galvanize changes in other groups. You will see the impact your narrative is having in terms of behavior changes, new kinds of action and new kinds of value created, all based on that contrast between the current background narrative and your new narrative. These are some of the ways you know your narrative has been taken on board and has developed a life of its own.

A note about control

Powerful and influential narratives can be built upon the mission, vision and values of a business, a social cause, even a product. But once the audience is invited in by the narrative's Initiator, and after Respondents begin to do their part and tell their own stories within the narrative, the boundaries of the narrative start to blur. Great narratives are flexible enough to include new voices. Their edges become meaningful territory in their own right.

Individuals and organizations cannot completely control the future scope of their narratives. With significant contributions from active Respondents and smaller contributions from relatively passive audience members, narratives are living entities with, so to speak, minds of their own.

Let's look at the role of narrative Initiator from a technology angle. Initiating a new narrative is much like launching an open-source software project. Most open-source efforts will have a core team that begins crafting a new software kernel. They then make it publicly available for interested users, testers and debuggers to play with and improve upon. Those "volunteer" code testers offer their patches, fixes and new code to the core team. From the many contributions, the core team selects those that further the core team's mission and the purpose of the kernel. Fundamentally, the software evolves over time and is strengthened by the contributions of many participants with diverse points of view and software skills. This was the strategy in 1991 used by Linus Torvalds, who began a project that later became the Linux kernel.

Applying open-source concepts to narrative, as Respondents of different stripes bring their values and experience to the narrative, they may argue with its intent or contribute their authority to validate or challenge its authenticity. They find ways to reframe its tenets for greater relatability. The Initiator of the narrative learns how Respondents embraced all this, including the call to action in the narrative, by what gets posted to social media, blogs and publications, and also by buying behavior.

To complete the analogy to open-source projects, even though the raw code is released into the wild, the Initiator of the code has an intention they are striving to achieve. To that end, open-source projects are decidedly not a democratic process. The Initiators build on contributions that take their project where they want it to go and ignore the contributions that go in other directions. To the extent the core code group has resources to harness community (Respondent) contribution in a focused way, they can very quickly guide the software to express their vision. Eric S. Raymond, one of the first observers of the nascent open-source movement, summed it up with what he called Linus' Law: "With enough eyeballs, there are no deep problems."

Likewise, if an Initiator of a narrative has enough resources to engage in a focused way with Respondents, they can amplify those contributions that further the intended messages and outcomes. The equivalent to Raymond's open-source quote applied to narrative might go like this: "With enough active storytellers working on a narrative, there is no worldview we can't sell to the public." The caveat here is that the narrative needs to be authentic or it will die on the vine before Respondents ever have a chance to amplify it.

In this way, narrative Initiators should think of themselves as stewards instead of storytellers. They should take their responsibility seriously to deliver, maintain and preserve the intention of a narrative. They should have the readiness and capacity to cultivate the narrative, including taking care of what you might think of as anchor stories at the center of the narrative. They may delegate delivery of those anchor stories to a collective of storytellers. Rather than simply being individual actors or directors of anchor stories, narrative Initiators set the stage for the new, keep track of what is emerging and "historify" the narrative as it grows, develops and evolves.

Whether you are a code jockey or an entrepreneur, a consultant or a marketing executive, you are a Respondent to the narratives around you. You are already a member of many narrative audiences, and have the opportunity to become an Initiator of those narratives that are most important to you. You have the opportunity to consciously craft your narrative with the constructs and tools you're learning about here.

The new audience — Respondents

Let's dig a little deeper into what it means to be a Respondent. Imagine the audience for a story as a group of people sitting at the feet of a writer. They listen eagerly to the tale as it builds to a climax and anticipate the resolution as the story ends. The audience is engaged, but it is made up of passive listeners taken on a mental and emotional journey by a commanding voice.

The audience for a narrative, on the other hand, includes listeners who are on their feet; they are actively responding and co-contributing. All are listening but many are ready to go beyond listening and become part of the process of expressing, evolving and amplifying the narrative. They feel connected to it. They are inspired to share it with other people and build on it. This audience can become an army of perpetual storytellers, and some will even initiate narratives of their own. They are Respondents.

A good example of this is the ALS ice bucket challenge, a gimmick that grew up around drawing attention to Lou Gehrig's disease and raising funds to fight it. This popular meme didn't actually originate from the ALS Association. Instead, it grew organically from golfer Chris Kennedy, who posted a video of himself pouring a bucket of ice water on his head and challenging his sister-in-law to do the same or donate to the ALS Association.

The challenge percolated through Kennedy's network and made its way to 30-year-old Pete Frates, a former college baseball player living with the muscle-wasting disease.[xv] Frates and his family turned out to be powerful catalysts for change. They responded strongly to this narrative. They pushed the challenge out into the world and helped make it one of the most viral memes of all time. From Frates, it spread like wildfire, inspiring civic-minded business and entertainment icons including Mark Zuckerberg, Bill Gates and Oprah Winfrey to post videos of themselves being doused with freezing water. According to the ALS Association, there have been 10 billion views of ALS ice bucket challenge videos. The group says that during the challenge's most viral time, over a six-week period in 2014, it raised $115 million.[xvi]

The narrative around the videos was clear — "be funny and go viral for a cause." It is almost endlessly entertaining to watch people cringe as the freezing water hits their head. And the narrative had a very clear call to action — each person, a Respondent, called out other people to take the challenge and respond in kind. It was tailor-built to be shareable and it connected deeply with people on several levels: Not only did it make them smile, but it made them want to contribute toward finding a cure for a terrible disease. Each person was doing something that felt very personal while also contributing to the broader narrative. The ALS ice bucket challenge pried Respondents up from passive-audience status to active participants.

The ALS ice bucket challenge was bold yet supple enough to contain stories critical of the challenge. Some called it "stunt philanthropy" and worried that the fun of the challenge had become more important than the cause. One writer at Time.com said the challenge was "problematic in every way."[xvii] But even such criticism of the challenge kept the focus on the intent of the narrative's Initiators to increase awareness of ALS and generate funding to work to end it. Critics weighing the merit of the ice bucket stories within the narrative helped to reinforce the narrative and thereby grew the audience of Respondents. Folks both for and against the intent of the narrative became part of an army of new Respondents, including storytellers and other narrative Initiators. Their differing interpretations of "truth" led these motivated Respondents to many unique actions and added richness to the original narrative.

In this chapter we have covered the difference between narrative and storytelling. We have also described the difference between narrative Initiators and Respondents and how the latter amplify elements of a narrative with their own stories. We've touched on how they may initiate new narratives of their own which may include counterpoints and different intentions than the original narrative. All of this serves to grow a narrative's impact. Along the way we outlined how the Initiator of a narrative has to relinquish control as their narrative takes on a life of its own. Ability to steer the evolution of a narrative is largely a matter of resources, but even those with nearly unlimited energy to throw at a narrative can be subverted by the public when certain nerves are pinched or if their narrative is revealed to be inauthentic.

Things to think about:

- What is the difference between the stories you find most compelling and the narrative behind them?
- In what narratives are you the Initiator? When are you are a Respondent? As a Respondent, did you tell your own story?
- What narrative can you identify that is clearly out of the control of its Initiator? What's happening to the narrative as a result? What is happening to the Initiator of the narrative?
- What narratives in your life have you initiated then had to give over to Respondents?
- How could you influence an army of Respondents that includes storytellers and more passive audience members?

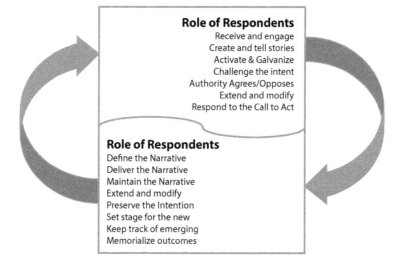

Role of Respondents
Receive and engage
Create and tell stories
Activate & Galvanize
Challenge the intent
Authority Agrees/Opposes
Extend and modify
Respond to the Call to Act

Role of Respondents
Define the Narrative
Deliver the Narrative
Maintain the Narrative
Extend and modify
Preserve the Intention
Set stage for the new
Keep track of emerging
Memorialize outcomes

CHAPTER 5

WANTED: AUTHENTIC, RELATABLE NARRATIVES WITH A CALL TO ACTION

FORCEFUL NARRATIVES NEED THREE things: They need to be authentic, they need to be relatable and they need to contain a call to action that the audience can respond to. We will cover how these fundamental elements are brought to life in a narrative in a subsequent chapter, but here we will examine how these three attributes work together to form the heart of a narrative.

Authenticity

In order to connect deeply to an audience, a narrative must be recognized by Respondents as authentic. But what do we mean by authentic? In the art world, authenticity can refer to the undisputed origin of a painting. In philosophy, authenticity means living a purposeful life. Authenticity is necessary to develop trust, whether that is between individuals, buyers and sellers, or between a narrative Initiator and their audience. It strengthens and sustains both the narrative and the Respondents in a symbiotic way. Authenticity also gives new narratives a fighting chance because it contrasts them from the background they emerge from. The evolution of an authentic narrative codifies, ushers in and supports new stories that amplify, modify or contest a given narrative. Authenticity provides the plausible credible grounding for all of this action to take place.

When we talk about authenticity in narrative, we are looking for three things:

1. Does the narrative make factually truthful claims?
2. Is the narrative credible for the individual or organization initiating it?
3. Does the narrative demonstrate some degree of vulnerability?

Let's take these one at a time.

Factually truthful claims

This sounds simple on the surface, but in the 21st century, when the new journalism can potentially make any clever person or group appear as a legitimate authority on a subject, it is not simple.

A good example of what happens when a company narrative is not built on factually truthful claims comes from POM Wonderful. Founded in 2002, the pomegranate juice company went all in on its narrative that drinking POM Wonderful could improve your health. In a series of ads, the company claimed that drinking POM Wonderful aided prostate and heart health. On its website, POM claimed that its juice could reduce hypertension, help cure erectile dysfunction and reduce the risk of cancer.[xviii]

The Food and Drug Administration took issue with POM, saying the company did not meet the administration's standards to make such claims. The Federal Trade Commission agreed and filed a complaint to force the company to stop making false claims about its juice. POM spent the next five years fighting the FTC in court. In January 2015 an appeals court in Washington, D.C., upheld the FTC's ban.[xix]

POM's problems didn't put the company out of business. But POM changed its marketing slightly to "Crazy Healthy" — enough to keep the FTC and FDA off of its back. The company's narrative was inherently inauthentic. While it claimed to be trying to shift behavior (drink more pomegranate juice to be healthier), it was allegedly manipulating perceptions by misleading people about pomegranate juice's health benefits.

Is the narrative credible?

How can you know what your Respondents will think is credible? What set of values are they measuring you against? Credibility means that the narrative is not just true on the surface, but that it reflects the deeply felt values of the Initiator. The narrative needs to be consistent with that individual's priorities. If a narrative springs from an organization, it must reflect the published values and mission of the organization as well as its actual operating practices.

This cannot be overstated: Authenticity will be gauged by how consistent your narrative is with what people know about your past performance or behavior, regardless of what you may have espoused as your values or priorities.

This raises two key points. First, people and organizations that are known for lying, cheating and stealing won't gain much of an audience because any stated narrative is bound to be contrary to the company's actual values. If your company makes inexpensive products, your narrative should not be one about luxury. If oil companies back your nonprofit, don't create a narrative around stopping climate change unless those companies are actually making a sincere effort to help the environment.

It is difficult (and expensive) to maintain an inauthentic narrative for very long. Remember, credibility will be gauged by what people know about your past behavior or performance. If all they know or remember is a string of missteps, it can take years to recover from such blows to credibility, whether they're deserved or not.

A great illustration of a credible and authentic narrative can be found at Patagonia, the outdoor clothing and gear manufacturer.

The day after Thanksgiving is traditionally known as Black Friday because of the crazy, sometimes dangerous sales that take place that day, when many people start their Christmas shopping. But since 2013, Patagonia has been hosting anti-Black Friday events, where the company encourages customers to get their jackets repaired instead of buying new ones.

This is very much in line with Patagonia's narrative of building quality products while helping the environment. Patagonia lives this narrative in every aspect of its business. The company has gone out of its way to be transparent about its supply chain — working with mills and factories to ensure that suppliers are implementing fair labor practices and doing all they can to mitigate their impact on the environment. Patagonia once ran an ad campaign with a picture of a cozy blue fleece and the words "Don't buy this jacket" in huge letters. Encouraging your customers not to buy is a daring move, but it enhanced the authenticity of Patagonia's narrative.

<u>Does the narrative demonstrate vulnerability?</u>

Creating a relatable narrative means digging deep, asking hard questions and potentially airing some uncomfortable truths. If you can be thoughtful, honest and open, you can find the truths that reveal what you are really all about and how hard you have worked to become that person or organization. That humility can help you develop a strong narrative. Communicating those truths shows that you or your organization is vulnerable, and that vulnerability helps your narrative be more relatable. Humans, by their very nature, are imperfect. A relatable narrative embraces that imperfection and invites our empathy, because we accept our own imperfections in the process. The call to action of the narrative helps show us a way to improve ourselves and the world around us.

When your organization has established trust with an audience, through being truthful, credible and vulnerable, the audience will be ready to accept and embody your narrative. That is why it is crucial that authenticity be viewed as a North Star when creating narrative. Whether by willful deceit or by negligence, inauthentic narrative is manipulation of perception. Respondents of all stripes eventually sense insincerity. Inauthentic narratives are usually like poorly executed magic tricks. The magician might try to create an aura of excitement and mystery, but all you see are the palmed aces and hidden pockets. Once the storytellers, the strongest allies of a narrative, discover it is bogus, they will turn all that storytelling power toward exposing the fraud. That has happened to many companies over the years. You can't afford that kind of press.

Deceitful narratives are almost always unmasked eventually. Narratives like Enron's famously failed investments, Bernard Madoff's Ponzi scheme and the home-mortgage frauds that led to the Great Recession grew to enormous proportions and eventually collapsed from the weight of their own inauthenticity. The fact that so few people were prosecuted for these crimes is a testament to the resiliency of narratives, however suspect, provided enough resources can be applied to keep them alive. Again, unless you have near infinite resources to maintain inauthentic narratives, it's better to err on the side of authenticity.

Relatability

It is very easy to embrace clichés and self-promotion when creating a narrative, but the problem with relying on those unsubstantial gestures is that they won't connect with anyone in a truly genuine way. Any company can make declarations about the superiority of its product or the originality of a concept. But those claims are hollow without a context that is reliable and that invokes the values and principles Respondents live by while offering some kind of aspiration. Individuals and organizations need to deliberately make their narratives relatable.

Relatability for a narrative must pass three tests:

- Is it contextual?
- Are values and principles presented?
- Are aspirations promoted?

We'll tackle these one at a time.

Is it contextual?

If a narrative is contextual, it reflects the time and place where and when it is created. If a narrative is out of sync with its era, it likely won't connect with many Respondents. That is not to say that some narratives aren't timeless — some are — but their expression must make sense in today's context. For example, the narrative of the "American Dream" has a history that predates the founding of the United States, but the expression of the American Dream narrative has evolved with the meaning of success in America. Likewise, narratives promoting the virtues of self-sufficiency will likely look and sound very different in Missoula, Montana, than they do in Midtown Manhattan. The narrative needs to make sense in a given geography, as well as a given era, for it to survive.

Let's explore the American Dream narrative a bit further, using Black Lives Matter again. The civil rights movement of the mid-20th century leaned heavily on the idea inherent within the narrative of the American Dream that everyone should have equal opportunities. But in 2015, that was not the right narrative to discuss the troubling trend of police killing unarmed black people. Fighting police brutality was part of the original civil rights movement, but the movement was more focused on efforts to change laws that treated black people as second-class citizens.

In 2015, Black Lives Matter took the key idea of the civil rights movement, equality, but put it into a modern context. It tapped a need. People were longing to find a meaningful way to connect what otherwise would have been seen as a string of unconnected instances of police brutality. Black Lives Matter created a narrative to connect stories from across the country. It also created a movement that took advantage of social media and other features of today's highly connected landscape to move people to take action.

Lastly, if a narrative is to thrive across a network of people, it will need to transcend geography and make sense to the members of that network regardless of location. Like Black Lives Matter, the Red Bull example used previously meets all of these context requirements very well, but in a totally different domain. For those who relate to it, Red Bull's extreme sports narrative helps Respondents define who they are (or are not) in relation to their peers and in relation to what was extreme in the past, what is extreme sport today and what may be coming.

Remember, a narrative takes its cues from the past but in order to be contextual, it must give meaning to the present. For your narrative to be contextual it must be of a specific place and time — the here and now. That doesn't always mean where you are physically. In today's connected world, physical location takes a backseat to a more intellectual orientation.

Does the narrative present values and principles?
The narrative needs to reflect your audience's values and priorities. If not, Respondents won't embrace it.

A great narrative touches something universal in many people at the same time. When we come in contact with a relatable narrative, it offers us a common perspective to help organize and understand ourselves and the world around us. That perspective is based around values and principles that we want to actualize in our lives. When a new narrative comes along that mirrors the things we hold dear (things like equality, an active lifestyle or a sense of personal empowerment), we are drawn to it. The pathway offered by the narrative has to resonate with the principles or rules we live by. If not, the narrative won't move us to act.

The only way to find those values is to understand the "why" of what you or your organization is trying to achieve. But too often, organizations focus their messages on the "what" and the "how" instead of the "why." When building a narrative, it is imperative that the "why" be loud and clear, even if you are a freelance worker building a business as an Uber driver or an Etsy shop owner. That "why" informs the narrative and gives you and your customers a deeper understanding of why your business exists and how it connects to what they value.

In order for a narrative to land that strongly, it still has to pass the authenticity tests we outlined above. It is not uncommon for narratives with great values and principles to fall on deaf ears because the Initiator of the narrative simply can't deliver it authentically. If the Initiator's actions and communication don't match, the narrative will be ineffective. A person or organization may publish a mission statement, vision and set of values to operate by, but if they don't live up to them, Respondents will spot that disconnect and avoid the narrative.

There are plenty of reasons, beyond narrative, for an organization to live its stated mission and values. Doing so makes the organization attractive to new employees and keeps existing stakeholders feeling like they are working toward a common purpose. And yet, organizations lose touch with their fundamental values all the time.

Maybe a business had an authentic mission at one time but the drive for profit overpowered those ideals. Perhaps an organization never had clear values to begin with and was just lurching from one difficult decision to the next without a clear path to guide it. Creating an authentic narrative will force you to understand the true values of your organization and whether they match your stated values. This is one of the most important benefits of understanding and cultivating an organizational narrative.

Revealing your organization's authentic self may seem daunting and difficult, and many don't want to make the effort because sometimes the truth hurts. But to set yourself apart, it's crucial to engage with your own organization's narrative at the deeper level we are unpacking here.

Is the narrative aspirational?

An important effect of narrative is that it invites and inspires Respondents to actively engage and participate in it. In the best cases, that engagement impacts Respondents' outlooks on life. "Just do it" is Nike's tagline, but it's also the company's narrative. It inspires Respondents to become better people and perpetuators of the narrative. Narratives like "Just do it" exert a force on communities. For example, Eugene, Oregon, where Nike was founded, is now "TrackTown USA."

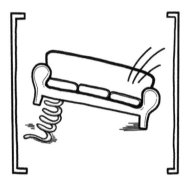

So "Just do it" is a successful, authentic narrative. But what happens when a narrative is inauthentic?

We saw clearly how disastrous that scenario can be in 2015 when the NFL tried to build a narrative that it was tough on players who were abusive at home. The football league has had a domestic violence problem for many years. Players' crimes were routinely swept under the rug or ignored so as not to interfere with the enterprise of football. An article on the website Deadspin showed that one team, the Seattle Seahawks, signed six different players with histories of domestic violence.[xx]

The problem came to a head when video surfaced of Baltimore Ravens running back Ray Rice apparently punching his girlfriend and then dragging her out of an elevator. A full five months later,

NFL Commissioner Roger Goodell announced that Rice would be suspended for two games as a punishment. After a huge backlash from the general public, Goodell suspended Rice indefinitely.

In order to try and repair some of the PR damage, the NFL partnered with an organization called No More and released a domestic violence public service announcement just before the 2015 Super Bowl. The ad was an attempt by the NFL to create a narrative that the organization puts women's safety above the needs of its teams. But the narrative was inauthentic. It tried to manipulate perception, so its call to action felt fake. Instead of changing people's perceptions of the sports organization, it ended up making the NFL look even worse.

The behavior of the NFL did not match the organization's narrative. That disconnect doomed the narrative. The stories that Respondents told around the narrative continued the damage being done to the NFL's reputation. Although it might feel hard, put the time and the energy into making sure your narrative is authentic. It will pay off in the long run.

Call to action

An authentic narrative has the power to shift behavior. Even if it is subtle, authentic narratives always contain a call to action. This call is crucial for your engaged audience to respond and participate. There are four main types of responses you can expect from a good narrative:

Mental: Your Respondents share new facts.

Emotional: Your Respondents have new feelings that they want to share.

Physical: Your Respondents change their behavior.

Economic: Your Respondents make new purchasing decisions.

A powerful example of a narrative with a successful call to

action is "Silence = Death."

In 1987, six gay activists plastered posters all over New York City of a pink triangle with the words "Silence = Death" at the bottom. The poster became the motto for ACT UP, the political action group founded by Larry Kramer that helped change the way the world thought about AIDS. At the time, the fear around AIDS was so extreme that there was talk of quarantining people with AIDS to keep the disease from spreading. People who were sick did their best not to talk about their illness and the disease was almost always a death sentence.

"Silence = Death" had a strong call to action. It inspired a cascade of profound behavioral changes. First, it encouraged those who were being quiet, either about their own illness or the illness of a loved one, to speak up. ACT UP showed the world that the disease could affect anyone but that it was difficult to transmit and that the people living with AIDS were real human beings who deserved all the help they could get. Government agencies started directing money and time toward coming up with a cure (or at least a way to prolong lives). Thus the narrative drove economic, research and other policy changes. People became more accepting of victims of the disease and people living with AIDS were able to find medical help and emotional support. Thus the narrative generated more empathy, an emotional shift across society.

"Silence = Death" was a relatable narrative. It was born from a place of anger and spoke to everyone's need to be heard. It was a contextual narrative. It spoke directly to that moment in time when by staying silent, people were destroying lives. It was also inspirational. It had a simple call to action — speak up. By refusing to stay silent, everyone was able to contribute and help to improve and save lives — a universal contribution that, at some level, we all aspire to make.

To wrap up this chapter on authentic, relatable narratives with a call to action, let's return for a moment to Patagonia's narrative, which is such a fine example. Patagonia has a long history of environmental concern and demonstrates this in its operations. The company is betting that most people have an inherent desire to do what they can to help the environment, and so can relate to Patagonia's narrative. This desire for environmental improvement is gaining more and more traction in the U.S. Patagonia's narrative is contextual. Today consumerism can feel out of control. We are pressured to buy, buy, buy, everywhere we go. Patagonia's ad message "Don't buy this jacket" gave people permission not to buy. What a refreshing and novel message. Finally, the narrative includes a call to action — do what you can to help the environment, even if that means not buying our company's products.

Paradoxically (or maybe not so paradoxically), this narrative has helped boost sales at Patagonia. Between 2008 and 2013, Patagonia (a private company) tripled revenue to $600 million.[xxi]

Things to think about:

- What are some companies or social causes that you admire? How do you know their narratives are authentic?
  - How can you tell if their claims are truthful?
  - Is the narrative credible for the individual or organization initiating it?
  - Does the narrative demonstrate some degree of vulnerability?
- Think about organizations whose narratives just don't pass the relatability test for you:
  - Are their narratives contextual? If not, why not?
  - Do their narratives present values and principles? Do they resonate with you?
  - What aspirations are they promoting? Are those your aspirations?
- Consider the last time you made a contribution to a nonprofit or a campaign, or perhaps you purchased

something because you believed in the narrative behind the product. What was the call to action that inspired your behavior?

○ What facts or figures made the difference for you?

○ How did the narrative make you feel or speak to your emotions?

○ What physical or behavioral changes did it inspire? How?

○ What about the narrative changed your spending or social patterns?

Participants Craft Perspective ...	Over Time.	
WHAT RESPONDENTS NEED:	Current	Emergent
Authenticity • Truthful claims • Credible for the Initiator • Demonstrates vulnerability		
Relatable Connections • Contextual • Values and principles • Aspirations		
Call to Action • Mental/facts • Emotional/feelings • Physical/behavioral • Economic/social		
TOOLS INITIATORS USE:	Current	Emergent
Nomenclature & Frames • Linguistic frames and assumptions • Special words • Story structure		
Resistance Honored • Opposing voices • Traditions and cultural mores • Other background inertia		
Inspiration Ignited • New path to a positive vision • New path to a problem solution • Personally inspiring • Communally inviting		
Stories Embedded • Valid and sincere • Connecting/relatable • Identifiable storyteller		

CHAPTER 6

NARRATIVE ANATOMY 101

LET'S GET A QUICK position fix on our path to understanding
narrative. So far, we've outlined what narrative is and how
narratives arise: A narrative is a thematic ecology of related,
contextual stories that inform and define one's perspective.
Narratives emerge as a force among participants crafting perspective
over time. Our main analogy for a narrative is a living mosaic made
up of thousands of tesserae that, taken together, reveal a grand
design. If the living mosaic is carefully built upon, the overall
impression is coherent, powerful and moving.

Ignited by resistance, narratives exist in a context of geography,
time and the rate of change of their era. They exist among a
community of narrators, storytellers and Respondents.

We've examined the conditions that give rise to the need for
consciously curated narratives, chief among them a 21st-century

reality: We are inundated with stories and tidbits of information yet have very few tools for finding meaning in it all. Narratives help us make sense of these stories and tidbits over time.

Whereas journalists and major news publications used to fill the role of curating information and packaging narratives for us, the Internet and social media have given rise to a "new journalism" that has displaced the old journalism. Now everyone is potentially a storyteller, narrative crafter and source of information. Whether all that new content is worthy of our trust is a major question we face daily. The "filter bubble" is a poor answer to this challenge and is largely a side effect of how Internet search algorithms have evolved. Importantly, most of us are not conscious of the filter bubbles we are creating. As we work on our computers, surf the Web and chat online with friends, we are not aware of the narratives we are experiencing and reacting to. This gives rise to two fundamental challenges for entrepreneurs and brand executives: 1) What narratives am I already responding to? and 2) Where do I put my energy and resources to get my audiences to respond positively to narratives I initiate amid all this noise?

From these questions we articulated the idea that a narrative must have drive: the dance between narrative Participants. We talked about the important roles that Initiators and Respondents play in crafting, evolving and sustaining narratives. These roles are fluid and, during the life of a narrative, Initiators and Respondents may play one or both roles, sometimes simultaneously.

Putting all these elements together, we can say that a discernable new narrative emerges as a force that will move people when context, meaning and drive work synergistically. A new narrative is initiated when it can be seen, heard and felt by Respondents, in contrast to a current background narrative. Often, but not always, that contrast presents itself in the form of resistance from the narrative audience. The more emotional energy a new narrative generates as a counterpoint to an incumbent narrative, the more it can be said to contrast against its background.

When a narrative becomes a living force that moves Respondents, they will report that it has three powerful attributes impacting them at the same time. First, the narrative will demonstrate authenticity, which the Respondents will recognize as containing truthful claims that are credible coming from the narrative Initiator. Second, Respondents will experience a relatable connection to the narrative. This means the narrative will be contextual, embody values and principles that resonate for the Respondents, and speak to their aspirations. Lastly, Respondents will recognize and be moved by the call to action embedded in the narrative. That call to action may generate in Respondents some combination of new ways of thinking, feeling, behaving, purchasing and/or engaging in society.

The last distinction to offer in this midpoint review is that narrative is necessary to keep up with the rate of change we are experiencing right now. In the 21st century, the world is moving faster than ever. We are on an accelerating exponential curve. For more than 5,000 years humans relied on horses. The steam era lasted only 150 years, and the era of the internal combustion engine is likely to give way to all-electric power in just over 100 years. Computing power doubles about every two years, in line with Moore's Law. Over our lifetime the population of the Earth has doubled. Change is no longer accelerating at a walk or trot that we can easily understand; it is accelerating at the speed of light, which we can barely visualize.

Today's rate of change, and the fact that it is accelerating, is why we need narratives more than ever. But not just any narratives — we need narratives that connect us to our communities and the things that make us all human. We need narratives that move us and make us respond and we need narratives that help us make sense of the almost overwhelming changes happening every day. Sure, for some people, narratives will simply be a way to sell more widgets. But if the narrative doesn't inspire something deeper and more human in your Respondents — a connection that is in shorter supply as we head up this steep curve — it will be ineffective regardless of your final goal.

To build successful narratives, it's first important to understand the narratives that are all around you and the ways you are responding to them, intentionally or absentmindedly. In this chapter, we will outline the tools that Initiators can apply to frame, craft, deploy, maintain and evolve narratives. The tools are:

- **Nomenclature and Frames:** This tool set includes linguistic frames — patterned language, special words and nomenclature — and story structure.

- **Honoring Resistance:** This tool set includes using opposing voices to create contrast, leveraging traditions and cultural mores, and taking advantage of other background forces.

- **Igniting Inspiration:** This tool set includes offering new paths to a positive vision, new paths to a problem solution, personally inspiring Respondents and inviting communal responses.

- **Embedding Stories:** This tool set includes stories that are valid and sincere, connecting/relatable, associated with identifiable storytellers, and with a clear story arc.

In this chapter, we will unpack each of these tool sets and use some examples so you can appreciate where they are being used and how. Our goal is not only to give you insights about the tools used to craft and deliver the narratives around you, but to show you the tools that are available to you for building your own narratives. In the next chapter we'll put it all into action.

Nomenclature and Frames

Linguistic frames

We previously invoked linguist and social scientist George Lakoff to help us define what we mean by "frame." He calls frames "mental structures that shape the way we see the world." They have a huge influence on narrative Initiators and Respondents. Once you understand the frame at the core of a narrative, it's like a light has been switched on in a dark room where you have been stumbling over furniture. Suddenly you can see how everything is arranged.

A good example of frame is the narrative around Lexus, Toyota's luxury brand. The "covenant" that Lexus dealers hold sacred is this: "Treat the customer as if they were a guest in your home."[xxii]

When Lexus launched its first model in 1989, it set a new standard for customer experience. They focused on the vehicle as a way to gain a customer; they focused on the customer experience to drive loyalty and keep customers. This was a breakthrough in the auto industry that changed the game for all of Toyota's and Lexus' competitors.

The "guest in your home" frame that the dealers had to take to heart and act on created an entire range of customer care responses.

The Lexus service experience became legendary. Lexus owners could have their cars picked up for service. If they did go to the dealership, the waiting rooms were beautiful and the car was never returned to the owner without first being washed and vacuumed. The frame of "guest" rather than customer made every employee a host instead of a supplier. The frame of "in your home" drove home the notion that the dealer cared about the customer as a person, not just as a transaction. Every mother at some point teaches every child that, when you have a guest in your home, the place better be clean, you always offer a refreshment and you do everything you can to make the guest comfortable, happy and glad they came by. The frame embedded in the Lexus covenant not only changed the industry in the late 1980s, but it forced Lexus to continue to stretch into new and relevant expressions of the narrative. The Japanese word for such hospitality, "omotenashi," is prominent on today's Lexus website.

The chosen frame must align with the intention of the Initiators. In the Lexus case, it did, and the company made a strategic breakthrough in the auto industry. Just like narrative, the frame has to pass Respondent tests that it is authentic and relatable and contains a call to action. The frame passed those tests but not just for one class of Respondents. It changed the game for dealers and their employees, for Lexus owners and new car prospects, and ultimately it changed the marketplace for every other auto manufacturer.

Patterned language, special words and nomenclature

All kinds of words have been made up by organizations and businesses with the intent to bring a narrative to life. One of the best examples comes from another automaker: Volkswagen. In 1990, the car company introduced an ad campaign featuring a stick figure graphic and a special word/tagline combo: "Fahrvergnügen: It's what makes a car a Volkswagen." As special words go, it was fun to say and fun to make fun of ("f-ing groovin'"). The word didn't have a terribly long life span (you won't find it in any of Volkswagen's contemporary marketing) but it was powerful at the time. It helped define Volkswagen's narrative of cars that are as much about fun as they are about reliability. It related to certain Respondents who wanted to live the Fahrvergnügen lifestyle and inspired new stories from people using the word in different contexts.

On the technology side, think about the word Xerox. Yes, it's the name of a company, but Xerox also managed to define an action: photocopying a document. Google did the same thing many years later around search. Turning your company's name (and therefore its brand) into a verb is one of the most powerful things a marketer can do.

While these words don't necessarily define each company's narrative, the creation of new words helps keep the companies in the conversation, even if only subtly. They also cement each company as a technological pioneer. If IBM had been first to the photocopying market, we might IBM all of our documents; if Yahoo had managed to hold on to search, we might Yahoo the name of that restaurant everyone is talking about. That status helps companies build new narratives.

Story structure

There's no question that stories are satisfying. We've been conditioned to expect a beginning, middle and end when we hear a story, and when that structure is disrupted, it can feel disturbing. Although stories aren't narrative, narratives are made up of stories and your Respondents will perpetuate your narrative through stories of their own. So it's important to keep story structure in mind when analyzing and creating new narratives.

When analyzing narratives, story structures can distract us from finding a narrative that is authentic and inspiring. Mass murders (more than four people killed, according to the FBI) in the United States are up. We all know the drill here. Activists on the left call for more gun laws. On the right, the NRA claims the government is coming for its members' guns. Politicians offer hollow condolences to the families of the victims and nothing gets done.

Each side takes comfort in its own story structure. Powerful narrative can help break down these barriers and effect change, which is why narratives can be so much more important than stories.

Honoring Resistance
Opposing voices

We've touched on the concept of opposing voices and resistance at several points in this work. These are common components of the contrast that every new narrative must have to distinguish itself from incumbent narratives. While opposition per se is not necessary, when there is an emotional component of a narrative's call to action, it often comes in the form of righteous indignation that the prevailing narrative must not stand a minute longer. That anger pushing against the current situation can only make sense if the current situation is pushing back, is opposing change. You can only have an argument if there are at least two sides. So, in order to change our consciousness, mode of being or behavior, we need to push off from something solid that represents the status quo we can no longer tolerate.

That leads us to a counterintuitive tool for building a narrative:

the idea that identifying resistance and setting up opposing voices is something desirable. The Initiator needs narrative Respondents to experience contrast. Going back to our living-mosaic metaphor, the artist's grand design is invisible if there is no visual contrast between the mosaic and the background in which it is laid.

Opposing voices can be identified for every authentic narrative that has a robust call to action. The most noble and long-lived narratives have counterpoints built into them. Consider the struggle of good versus evil [that is at the core of Christian, Jewish and Islamic narratives. The Satan figure in each tradition provides the opposing voice for the narrative of a virtuous life. As Respondents to these pervasive narratives in the West, we have the good/evil duality on board and are bombarded with it in every TV show, movie and nearly every news feature we see or hear. Most young children believe that the world is a good place full of grownups who have their best interests at heart. But that's not always true, and in order to get by in the world, children have to slowly realize that there is more danger out there than they see with their youthful eyes.

"The world is a dangerous place pushes back against their naive notion that the world is safe. And it is that pushback that makes being virtuous something we can identify, by contrast, as desirable.

It's the unspoken tagline to the golden rule that gives it meaning: "Do unto others as you would have them do unto you ... *or bad things will happen.*"

Let's tie this back to narratives we've discussed above. The resistance to Nike's "Just do it" narrative is our own laziness. For most of us, the opposing voice is our inner Homer Simpson, who reminds us, "Hey buddy, not doing it is way easier than just doing it. Here, have a doughnut." That inner sloth wants us to sit on the couch and skip the exercise in favor of binge-watching our favorite TV series. It's easy to plan for our much healthier, fitter future. It's harder to take the initiative to exercise right now. "Just do it" helps push us off of the couch and out the door. It helps overcome our internal opposing voice.

In the "Silence = Death" story, the voice of resistance came from our culture's ignorant fear of a disease it didn't understand. You may recall when basketball star Magic Johnson announced that he was HIV positive. His declaration sent shockwaves through the NBA, and fellow players were afraid to play with and against him. Until a few first followers stepped up to support Johnson's educational efforts, the opposing voices for the new narrative he was supporting were nearly overwhelming. That much resistance, however, put the HIV narrative into high relief against an incumbent, albeit ignorant, perspective. That contrast ultimately gave the narrative around solving the important social and public health challenges of HIV enormous power that circled the globe.

Traditions and cultural mores

Whether a narrative passes the contextual test described in the previous chapter will, to some degree, depend on the traditions and cultural mores of the geography and era in which the narrative is attempting to take root. Narratives that survive long enough ultimately generate traditions and cultural mores, and in that regard become self-perpetuating. Let's take, for example, the narrative of innovation that swirls around Silicon Valley. Over the last 40 years, Silicon Valley has become synonymous with innovation and increasingly novel business models in the technology sector. Stories of pairing venture funders with entrepreneurial Stanford

University technology students are legendary in Silicon Valley. Such extracurricular opportunities are part of the mystique surrounding Stanford and the narrative around attending (and graduating from) that institution.

Books have been written about the cultural mores of "the Valley" and how they enable innovation, among them "The Rainforest" by Victor Hwang and Greg Horowitt and "The Rainforest Scorecard" by Henry Doss and Alistair Brett. These authors point out how the traditions and culture of Silicon Valley reduce "transactional friction," making it easier to do business with partners, colleagues, customers and suppliers with minimal formality.

They attribute the much higher volume and velocity of new business starts in Silicon Valley to six classes of factors that favor innovative behaviors in 1) the local culture, 2) leadership across companies and communities, 3) frameworks for innovation, 4) resources directed at innovation, 5) activities across the region that highlight innovation and 6) a celebration of role models of innovation. All of those features in concert improve capacity for further innovation because innovative behavior is a norm, not an anomaly — the narrative is self-reinforcing.

The narrative about Silicon Valley is so compelling that cities all over the United States, and indeed the rest of the world, are doing what they can to emulate the traditions and cultural mores found in the Bay Area. There's Silicon Alley in New York City and Silicon Hills in Austin, Texas. The U.S. Department of Commerce is doing what it can to understand the traditions and culture of Silicon Valley so that it can facilitate more innovation-based economic development, especially in distressed communities across the country. Shifting traditions and cultural mores toward generative narratives is no small feat, but with the acceleration provided by the "new journalism," generative narratives can spread faster than ever.

<u>Other background forces</u>

Most authoritative works shy away from buckets titled "other background forces" because it doesn't sound very smart or, frankly, all that useful. However, in the case of narrative, since we are really talking about a living system of culture, traditions, ideas, stories, words, images and so on, one must keep in mind that this is fuzzy. Even though we have broken narrative down into its constituent parts, including context, meaning and drive, it's still a messy business. We've outlined the participants, including Initiators, who have tools to work with in launching and crafting narratives, and Respondents who want narratives to have authenticity, relatable connections and a call to action. Even so, there is tremendous diversity in the way those roles are expressed and interchanged between players.

It is fundamentally important to approach narrative with the wonder, curiosity and open-mindedness that you had when you first started reading, because "other background forces" are what happen while you're busy making other plans. For example, whatever narrative was being pursued to improve New Orleans during the first week of August 2005 was completely irrelevant by the last week of that same month. Hurricane Katrina initiated a flood of new narratives and washed away as many more. You may recall that the Federal Emergency Management Agency took years to recover its narrative of responsibility and responsiveness after the debacle that was FEMA's performance post-Katrina.

Beyond extreme weather, there are many kinds of events that quickly change the context for narratives, and in so doing favor some and destroy others. In the destructive sense, all manner of natural disasters can affect ecologies and human infrastructure; then there are acts of terrorism and war, major crimes and mass murders. There are plenty of examples of narratives that became regional conflagrations after a trigger event that was not planned.

"Twenty-six-year-old Mohamed Bouazizi, living in the provincial town of Sidi Bouzid, had a university degree but no work," reports The Guardian. "To earn some money he took to selling fruit and vegetables in the street without a license. When the authorities stopped him and confiscated his produce, he was so angry that he set himself on fire."[xxiii] Within days, the Tunisian Revolution began what ultimately became known as the Arab Spring.

Significant geopolitical changes resulted from one man's act of desperation which turned into riots and regime changes across much of the Middle East and North Africa. In some cases, protests became civil wars; in others, national leaders were unseated; but in all cases, the new narrative of change was amplified by the new journalism outlined in the previous chapter. The trigger event lit the match to tinder that was just waiting to burn. As the Arab Spring conflagrated, the context for incumbent leaders and incumbent narratives changed completely. The new narrative swept away the incumbent rulers of Tunisia, Egypt, Yemen and Libya in less than 24 months.

Igniting Inspiration

Not all narratives have grand geopolitical implications. Not all narratives need to spark a transformative cause. However, some narratives are so compelling and simple, in a generative way, that they inspire small acts of self-improvement in the Respondents, which, when put together, can create a healthier society.

New path to a positive vision

To explain what we mean, let's look again at Nike's "Just do it" campaign. An Adweek story commemorating the 25th anniversary of the campaign called it "the last great tagline in advertising history."[xxiv] "Just do it" started out as an ad campaign but became the narrative of Nike. From Adweek:

"Just do it" was one of the biggest ad ideas ever, destined to cut across all conceivable psycho/socio/demographic lines in ways author Dan Wieden couldn't have envisioned when he tossed off the phrase in 20 minutes, concerned that the initial half-dozen ads in the campaign, spotlighting various subjects and different sports, had no unifying message.

Simplicity is really the secret of all "big ideas," and by extension, great slogans. They must be concisely memorable, yet also suggest something more than their literal meanings. Rather than just putting product notions in people's minds, they must be malleable and open to interpretation, allowing people of all kinds to adapt them as they see fit, and by doing so, establish a personal connection to the brand.

Slogans are not necessarily narratives, but in this case, the "big idea" ticked all of the boxes that you need to construct a narrative. "Just do it" assembled many different stories into a meaningful whole. It reflected the company's values and mission. It was relatable: We all have a desire to take action instead of just sitting back. It was contextual: Although the narrative is now more than 25 years old, it is flexible enough to continue to evolve along with changing sports fads. As people have taken on the slogan as their personal mantra for self-improvement, their stories have become personalized parts of the collective narrative. "Just do it" was also inspiring. There were no more excuses for inaction.

Nike values the idea that anyone can be an athlete. The most talented, highest-paid athletes in the world wear their shoes. But so do kids playing in the cul-de-sac. No matter your shape, size, ability or age, Nike wants to be on your feet, and because of Nike's strong narrative, wearing Nikes inspires you to connect with your inner athlete. "Just do it" not only accurately reflects the company's values and imbues the narrative with meaning, it commands us all to be our best selves.

New path to a problem solution

Beyond inspiring us to achieve our potential, narratives help us focus to solve problems. In the movie "Apollo 13," based on the real space drama that played out in 1970, NASA Flight Director Gene Kranz responds to the unfolding danger with the line "We've never lost an American in space, we're sure as hell not gonna lose one on my watch. Failure is not an option!" "Failure is not an option" is a pretty good summation of NASA's narrative. As you consider the problems you or your organization are facing, how do the narratives in your life help you solve those problems?

There are corporate narratives that rival NASA's and get

tested just as harshly. Swagelok is an Ohio-based company that manufactures precision fittings, tubing and assemblies used by the chemical and energy industries. When the giant earthquake and tsunami hit Japan in March 2011, radioactive water leaking out of the area around the Fukushima nuclear plant created an ongoing emergency situation.

AVANTech, an industrial water-treatment company, was called in to design a system to keep the water from reaching the city and the ocean. The firm turned to Swagelok for the tubing, valves and fittings it needed to quickly build its system.

Swagelok's narrative is one of quality and reliability. That strong and authentic narrative helped AVANTech solve its problem. Swagelok had people working overtime and on weekends to put the order together. When the order arrived and the goods proved to be 100 percent reliable, AVANTech President James L. Braun had a strong reaction:

"And the one thing I want to say is, and I do get emotional with some of this, Fourth of July, we're here shipping this equipment and we make a phone call. The Swagelok parts were here on the Fourth of July. Most people are out grilling, or partying, or doing their thing. And you say, 'We need these parts,' and we got them. So, that's a big deal." [xxv]

When one of those "other background forces" created a tsunami that took out a nuclear power plant, it created an opportunity for the company based on Swagelok's integrity narrative.

Narratives that support relentless and vigorous problem-solving remind us of our ability to stay cheerful and resourceful in the face of adversity. They keep the assumption close to the surface that there is no puzzle, challenge or obstacle too big, too complex or too foggy for the human mind to address and ultimately solve.

Personally inspiring

Inspiration comes in many forms; some are much more subtle than heroic, and much more about influencing purchases than solving the global threat of a nuclear reactor breach. Apple's "Think different" campaign inspired people to be more creative with their electronics. Eventually that tagline grew into a narrative about personal identity: "Are you a Mac or a PC?" For years, carrying a Mac laptop was a statement of identity that said, "I'm part of the creative class."

Nike's drive is to get its shoes on people's feet so they will "Just do it." The more people Nike inspires to see themselves as athletes and the more people that value physical fitness, the more shoes Nike will sell. Nike values the idea that everyone can be an athlete, and that all starts with getting off the couch and doing something physical, whether that's running, playing tennis or going for a walk in the park. To do those things, you need shoes. If the "Just do it" narrative is what made you decide to start moving in the first place, chances are you'll buy a pair of Nikes.

It's important to note that Nike is not saying to get out there and become a professional athlete. "Just do it" is broadly inspiring and flexible enough to apply to many different fitness levels. It doesn't criticize you if all you plan to do is walk around the block. If you had to push yourself even a little to do that, you are embraced by the "Just do it" idea.

Inviting communal responses

Narratives that are truly robust engage entire communities, not just individuals. Barack Obama structured his 2008 presidential campaign around the narrative of "Yes, we can." A variation of the "Sí se puede" rallying cry that united farmworkers around Cesar Chavez in 1972, "Yes, we can" brought together a majority of voters despite a tremendous diversity of age, race, gender and region. Not only did "Yes, we can" speak to the problem of underrepresentation of people of color in American politics — it invoked a spirit of uniting at a time when politics have felt deeply divisive. Regardless of how you voted in the 2008 election, it is hard to deny the power that campaign had to invite broad participation.

A narrative for donors and parents

During the day, Roger Tsai sets the roadmap for personalization and analytics at Gracenote, a company that maintains a massive database of music metadata. But in his off-hours, Tsai sits on the board of Camp Phoenix, an immersive summer program for low-income youths. Like any nonprofit, Camp Phoenix needed funding to get off the ground in 2012.

As a founding director, Tsai employed narrative to help focus the camp's message and facilitate discussions with donors. "I wanted to open doors, evangelize and figure out who in the community might prove helpful," says Tsai. "Creating a strong narrative helped us do that."

Tsai needed a narrative that would attract both donors and campers. His board settled on: "An academic summer camp for urban youth."

"There are many different ways we could have described the camp, but this had the most resonance," says Tsai. "It generated the most momentum."

Having the word "academic" was important because the camp helps students avoid the learning loss that can result from an idle summer. At the same time, Camp Phoenix is very much a camp, complete with swimming and night hikes. The narrative was flexible enough to encompass all of the stories that make up Camp Phoenix while inspiring a call to action. For donors, that call was to give money. For parents, that call was to send their kids to the camp.

Tsai credits the narrative with the camp's success. They've been able to increase the number of campers by 50 percent each year and have received funding from organizations like the Golden State Warriors. "It's so important to communicate what you're setting out to do in those early days," says Tsai. "You can get them on board or you can lose them, depending on how you frame your narrative."

The approach Tsai took to Camp Phoenix's narrative invited the community of parents, kids, funders and others to participate. In so doing, the Camp Phoenix call to action brought people together around a wholesome mission and a specific place.

Embedding Stories

Stories are a crucial part of any narrative. Without them, a narrative is just an idea. Stories bring the narrative to life and give Respondents something to hold on to, share and create. For stories to successfully promote a mission, they should have three main attributes. First, the stories need to be valid and sincere. Second, stories should be connecting and relatable. Third, every story needs an identifiable storyteller. When a story has all three attributes working in the service of a narrative, it can be a very powerful contributor in the life of the narrative.

Valid and sincere

Stories that are accidently untruthful or deliberately misleading will sooner or later be exposed. This does tremendous damage to the narrative the stories arose from. So what happens when there is a disconnect between a narrative and one of its key stories?

Restaurant chain Chipotle is a company that has struggled mightily with this question over the past year. Most fast food restaurants focus on price and speed — the cheaper and quicker, the better. But Chipotle has helped to change the fast casual game with its narrative of serving "food with integrity." The chain tries to live that narrative in every aspect of operations. Whole ingredients are used in the kitchen, where food is cooked instead of just defrosted and fried. Meat and vegetables are sourced only from suppliers that meet the highest standards of quality and responsibility to the land, animals and the environment.

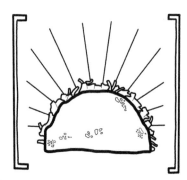

At least that has been Chipotle's intention. Over the past year, the chain has been plagued by stories of people getting ill after eating at the restaurant. Over six months, people in at least 11 states were sickened by E. coli from eating at Chipotle. Then a different food-borne illness sickened diners in Boston.

Chipotle founder Steve Ells apologized and promised that Chipotle was committed to "becoming known as the leader in food safety."[xxvi] That did little to calm investors and customers who began to associate Chipotle with stomach illness. Eventually, Ells took the major step of closing all Chipotle stores for one day to discuss food safety with his employees.

It remains to be seen if this can get Chipotle back to its previous level of popularity. Investors initially seemed somewhat satisfied. Between Feb. 8 (the day the restaurants closed down) and Feb. 19, stock climbed 14 percent to $511. That's still well off the company's 52-week high of $758.61 — but it's a start.

Chipotle still has some hard work ahead of it to bring the company back in line with its narrative. But the company's actions are a good start. Chipotle's narrative isn't suddenly inauthentic because of its recent woes. But the stories being told about the company have completely disconnected from the narrative. That's a difficult situation for any company.

<u>Connecting and relatable</u>

Refining our theme that authentic and relatable narratives require authentic and relatable stories, we observe that the stories in the strongest narratives have a way of connecting to Respondents that uniquely fits their everyday needs as well as their more abstract values. To make the strongest impact among your targeted Respondents, present your stories, and thereby your narrative, in a way that fits naturally into their lifestyle. Sometimes just putting your story inside the right physical setting is all it takes to make a powerful connection.

Grameen VidaSana is a health care center in Queens, New York, that works with (mostly migrant) women in the Jackson Heights neighborhood. The center was built with the best of intentions: to give women in the community the tools they need to improve their own health. When it opened, the center offered things like weight-loss clinics and diabetes education, but there was one problem — women weren't showing up.

Ibanga Umanah's consulting firm, Jump Associates, stepped in to help the clinic connect with its community. Jump consultants observed local women for several weeks and listened to their stories. They chatted with them about things like money and raising children.

What they found was that the clinic's message didn't connect because it wasn't aligned with the way the women lived their lives. They didn't want to follow a curriculum pushed on them from people outside the community. They wanted help with their goals, but on their own terms.

"We look for the rules people are living by and what the larger viewpoints are that connect those stories," says Umanah. "We call those frames." But, as you've learned, we could call it narrative.

Umanah's team found that the women were very interested in taking care of themselves, but that usually meant getting a facial or a manicure. "The feeling is that 'When I look good I feel strong and healthy,'" says Umanah. "Something like going to the beauty salon is a way of taking care of yourself."

With this new understanding, the clinic changed its approach to the community. It offered things like free facials to get women in the door and then talked to them about preventative care.

By identifying the narratives that define the women and their lives, and noticing specifically how those narratives are expressed in behavior, Umanah was able to help the clinic attract more patients. By repositioning the Grameen VidaSana narrative and its stories to sync with Respondents' existing behavior, the clinic was able to express its mission more successfully.

Identifiable storyteller

For narratives and the stories within them to pass our internal tests for authenticity and relatability, we always want to know who is speaking. We can't gauge credibility if there is no byline under a news item. There is no way to begin to know if the story is worth assessing for validity if we don't know where it comes from. In the case of testimonials and referrals about a product, service or individual, the "who" making the statement is as important as what they are saying.

In organizational settings, the CEO is the most easily identified storyteller; their every word is scrutinized. A chief executive's story and narrative skills can determine the success, or failure, of the organization.

Recall the story about Swagelok and the Japanese tsunami. Swagelok's CEO, Art Anton, leads that multibillion-dollar manufacturing enterprise with steely operational efficiency, but also with a deeply personal commitment to his people and the company's customers. Anton is not a flamboyant, outspoken CEO, but his frequent delivery of the company's values is crisp, clear, consistent and compelling, whether he is addressing hundreds of distributors, thousands of employees or customers from around the world. And when Anton orders the company to mobilize around an international nuclear crisis that can be solved by a mountain of precision plumbing fixtures and stainless steel tubing — well, that generates a story where the speaker is an undisputed leader.

As that story gets retold inside Swagelok and among its customers, you can bet that it contributes to the company narrative around customer focus, quality, integrity, respect, continuous improvement and innovation. It also increases Anton's credibility as a leader.[xxvii]

Organizational storytelling is not always so powerful and generative. An organization's narrative can be challenged when new leadership takes over. An entire company might be aligned behind one narrative, and then a new CEO steps in with a very different point of view.

"Narrative in its truest sense should be evergreen," says Grace Angulo, a senior vice president at Edelman public relations. "But the leadership team really needs to have a stake in the ground and some ownership over the narrative."

Sometimes the change in leadership coincides with the need for a new narrative. J.C. Penney was in terrible shape in 2011 when the company hired Ron Johnson from Target to take over as CEO. Johnson, a former Apple executive, changed the narrative of Penney from a place with lots of sales to a store defined by everyday low prices.

But the new narrative didn't work. It didn't reflect what loyal shoppers liked about the company, and sales slumped even further. Two years after taking over, Johnson was replaced.

If new leadership demands a new narrative, the organization should follow the framework outlined in this book and the steps in the following chapter. That includes a new leader empowering workers in the organization to be vulnerable and honest about problems that the leadership may not see or hear. Are the leaders being honest with themselves about what's working and what isn't? The stories floating around the organization (or in the media) of failure to deliver on a company narrative are as important to examine as any good news story. And equally important: Who is telling and spreading those stories? Are the sources identifiable and credible? Are those sources being taken seriously even if they are just spreading rumors?

A narrative illustrated by powerful stories that are authentic and inspiring can help motivate individual, organizational and, indeed, national performance. But keep in mind that, as leaders change, they can introduce new risks to narratives. To reinvoke our living-mosaic metaphor, if a new master artist comes on-site and tries to impose his vision on a design that is well-established, especially without a collaborative dialogue to bring fellow artists and Respondents along, the mosaic design can be thrown into disarray. In organizations, tremendous damage can be done to the external brand and internal culture if new leaders are insensitive to the living narrative and stories that already exist. On the other hand, when fresh leadership identifies and engages respected internal and external storytellers to refresh a well-crafted narrative, that act can lead to huge and generative changes. The respected and inspiring personalities who are telling the stories become embodiments of the new narrative.

Things to think about:

- What narratives in your personal or professional life are important to you?
- What frames and special nomenclature put boundaries around those narratives?
- What stories get repeated over and over in your family? At your work? Why do they recycle and what behaviors do they engender?
- Can you identify the opposing voices or resistance in those narratives that gives you something to push against? How do those voices increase the contrast so your narratives are clear?
- How do the traditions and mores in your family or workplace reinforce incumbent narratives? What traditions are forming that support new narratives? Are they healthy and generative?
- When have major surprises, whether a natural disaster or man-made calamity, changed everything for you? What breakthrough opened major new possibilities?
- How has a narrative inspired you to take action to improve your personal or work life? When has that been some

communal action?

- What stories have made the most difference for you? What narrative(s) do they roll up into?
- Are there other metaphors and analogies that help you understand narrative?

CHAPTER 7

KNOW THY NARRATIVE, THEN IMPROVE ON IT

NOW THAT YOU HAVE a sense of some constructs for making sense of narratives, and you're getting the idea that you are responding to and initiating narratives (sometimes simultaneously), it's time to put all those ideas into action. In this chapter we'll assemble the constructs into procedures you can use to analyze your narratives and improve upon them. The tools and processes in this chapter are organized according to level of depth and detail. You can choose the tools that match how deep you want to go with your narrative analysis and narrative initiation.

The narrative models can be operated at three levels. Instructions and worksheets for each level follow:

1. **Minimum Narrative Formula**

    This tool is designed to very quickly help you examine some "content in question" to determine if it is a narrative or something else. This tool will also help you rough out a new narrative very quickly now that you've gotten some familiarity with the narrative model. If you only have an hour to play around with this topic, fill out the template and have a conversation about it with colleagues. You'll get some great insights to work with and you'll learn a ton.

2. **Narrative Scorecard**

   This tool is designed to help you systematically assess the completeness, context, meaning and drive of a given narrative. The 26 questions can be responded to with numerical scoring for a relatively thorough but fast assessment of a narrative's strengths and weaknesses. This will also reveal how much you know about the content in question and whether it is, in fact, a narrative or not. If you have half a day, you can work through this with a group and still have time for a coffee break. However, the questions in this section invite you to look much deeper and write descriptive responses to build out your narrative assessment in depth. If you are considering a new branding project for your organization, a major new product launch or something of that magnitude, it will be well worth your time to use this tool and work in depth.

3. **Narrative Design Session Series**

   This section will give you the outline of a series of Narrative Design Sessions that 21st Century Narrative can conduct for your organization. This section will lay out the major questions we would tackle with you if we were guiding you through a robust narrative assessment and initiation. We won't get into all the details here of each Narrative Design Session, but you'll have enough to get a sense of what's involved. The questions will guide you, if you wish to undertake this work on your own, generally through the flow we use. We always custom-design such work according to client needs, but this outline will give you a good generic starting point. A series of design sessions of this type might be collapsed to a few days or conducted over a period of weeks depending on the scope, scale and pace of your project.

What do we assume about you, dear reader, as we offer these tools? We assume you have read the previous chapters of this book, and that you will fearlessly adapt the questions in these generic tools to fit your situation, goals and the depth to which you are ready to go. Call us as questions come up.

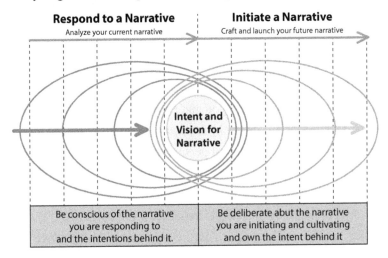

Respond to a Narrative	Initiate a Narrative
Analyze your current narrative	Craft and launch your future narrative

Intent and Vision for Narrative

Be conscious of the narrative you are responding to and the intentions behind it.	Be deliberate abut the narrative you are initiating and cultivating and own the intent behind it

Minimum Narrative Formula

Purpose

This tool provides a process for simply and quickly thinking through the most basic elements of an existing narrative or, alternatively, sketching out those basics for a new narrative. It helps you:

1. Remember the most basic narrative elements and their logic to form a basic narrative.
2. Consistently return to the same narrative structural elements so that you don't get lost in rambling conversations about a narrative without articulating it as a whole system.
3. Get meaningful insights from narrative analysis or substantive progress on a narrative initiation when you have very limited time and attention to get it done.

Participants

This tool can be used by individuals or groups for personal or organizational narratives. In the case of individual narrative, it is useful to fill out the form as if you were a friend filling it out about you. Putting yourself in the shoes of an external observer is challenging, but well worth it. If you can get some help from someone who has observed you and your narrative for some time, that's even better. In life we have plenty of opportunities to work our narratives from an internal perspective, but few people really objectively examine such deeply personal topics with outside input.

In the case of organizational narrative, this is somewhat easier, but still challenging. To get the most rounded perspective on organizational narrative, do the analysis or new narrative initiation with as diverse a team as you can. If this work is left only to executives (marketing or otherwise), the narrative analysis or initiation will likely overlook deeply rooted organizational issues. The executive roles all too often insulate even the most well-meaning leaders from many organizational realities. Authentic narratives require more depth and breadth of perspective than leaders generally have in isolation.

Process

The process for this tool is simply to complete each sentence. This is an internal document, so you don't have to worry about wordsmithing — this is just for developing clarity. Here are some pointers about each section in the template:

1. **Title and Context**

   a. Title — Naming your narrative (the content in question) is just to make it easy to refer to, and whatever name you give it now can be changed. What will you call this narrative?

   b. Context — Fill in whatever context boundaries are relevant for your narrative (dates, geography and network of people). How do you contextualize this narrative?

2. **About the Initiator**

   a. Initiator — If this is a personal analysis, you may be the Initiator, but in organizations there may be more than one Initiator (and some may be outside the organization, especially if communications, public relations or ad agencies are involved). Who are they?

   b. Values — This question asks, in the simplest terms, what values or priorities the Initiator is trying to satisfy. What Initiator values and priorities does this narrative attempt to satisfy?

   c. Intention — The intention of the narrative describes specific objectives that serve those Initiator values. Make a statement of intent for this narrative.

3. **About the Respondents**

   a. Respondents — Whether you are working a personal or an organizational narrative, there will be more than one

Respondent. How much time you have for this exercise will determine how broadly you consider the Respondents of any given narrative. Who are they?

b. Values — This question asks, in simplest terms, what values or priorities the Respondent is trying to satisfy. What different Respondents want a real bearing on how they engage with a narrative? What are the values and priorities your Respondents are working to satisfy?

4. **Opposing Voices**

a. Opposition — This question addresses a specific type of Respondent that will resist the narrative's authenticity, context, relatability or specifically its call to action. For individuals, that resistance comes from inside. Again, when examining your own narratives, try to take a third-person perspective and treat your inner "loyal opposition" as if it were a part of yourself. For all other narratives, the opposing voices may be internal to the initiating organization or outside it. Who are those opposing voices?

b. Values — Whether the opposing voices are internal or external, what values and priorities are trying to be satisfied by the resistance these voices are putting up?

5. **Stories**

a. Stories — Every narrative includes at least one story, but usually many, that describes the difference or journey between the current set of assumptions, beliefs, aspirations and linguistic frames and a new set. It may take several stories to cover all the bases. Some of those stories may be so familiar that they aren't even considered special, they're just "how I am" or "how we operate." Those expressions of culture are very important to capture.

b. Related Stories — For a narrative to be well-formed, the stories within it will share some connecting threads, themes or elements. That's how we know they are all rolling up under the same narrative umbrella. Articulate those commonalities among the stories.

6. **Inspiration and Call to Action**
   a. Actions Inspired — What are the Respondents moved to do?
   b. Actions Inhibited — What are the Respondents dissuaded from by embracing this narrative?
   c. Other Value or Changes — What else do Respondents get from embracing this narrative?

7. **Generative Versus Regressive Narrative**
   a. Generative Narrative — To make the world a better place, the narratives you embrace and initiate must be generative. Ask yourself how the narrative in question supports sustainability (environmental, social and economic) and realization of human potential.
   b. Regressive Narrative — There are plenty of narratives that don't make the world a better place and amplify our weaknesses, prey upon our vulnerabilities and leave us in fear. How is this narrative an "opposing voice" to regressive narratives? Which specifically?

8. **Linguistic Frames and Nomenclature and Special Words**
   a. Linguistic Frames — Given all that you've unpacked about this narrative so far, what is the most basic assumption this narrative makes? What are a few words for expressing that?
   b. Nomenclature and Special Words — What is the unique lingo for this narrative?

Products/Outcomes

This narrative overview can produce a one-page brief or the table of contents for a detailed effort.

Minimal Narrative Formula

1a	This narrative (the content in question) is **entitled** ...
1b	This narrative lives in a **context** defined by: (date range) (geography) (network)
2a	The **Initiator**(s) of this narrative is/are:
2b	who **value** ...
2c	The **intention** behind this narrative is to ...
3a	The **Respondents** of this narrative are:
3b	who **value** ...
4a	This narrative generates **opposing voices** (internal and/or external) such as:
4b	who **value** ...
5a	This narrative includes **stories** about ...
5b	which are **related** because they all ...
6a	This narrative **inspires** Respondents to **take actions** such as ...
6b	and **inhibits** Respondents from actions such as ...
6c	The **other value or changes** that are generated for Respondents over time are:
7a	This narrative is **generative** because it supports sustainability and the realization of human potential ...
7b	This narrative **counters regressive** narratives that diminish sustainability and inhibit humanity by ...
8a	The linguistic **frames** embedded in the narrative include:
8b	The **nomenclature** and **special words** include:

Narrative Scorecard — Part I Quantitative

Purpose:

This tool provides a process for assessing how well-formed a narrative may be. It helps you:

1. Develop your ability to recognize narratives and their components in action.
2. Prepare you to quantitatively analyze narratives to which you are a Respondent.
3. Prepare you to intentionally develop narratives for which you are the Initiator.

Participants:

You can certainly use this tool as an individual. As a journaling activity to unpack the narratives that run your life, this tool is an incredibly powerful exercise. Just giving a little thought to the narratives that are swirling around your workplace, your home life and your community will be very enlightening. From this introspection you will gain a much stronger sense of how you are impacted by the narratives in your environment. While the questions are worded for business and organizational settings, with a little thought you can rephrase them for individual purposes. It's much more art than science, so have at it.

Ideally, this assessment is conducted as a group exercise. Once the content in question is identified and titled (as instructed below), a group can work the assessment questions for both scoring and written responses. If the content in question is internal to an organization, the group will gain a powerful shared understanding of very intangible aspects of organizational culture, perspectives, stories and so on. If the content in question is external — say, about a specific competitor or market or an emerging market need — the group can apply discipline to what is often considered pure "agency insight," which is, well, magical.

Process:

1. **To begin, identify the "content in question" you want to assess, and give it a name.**

   You may refine the name after you've done your analysis, but the content in question must be titled so you can keep in mind the boundaries of what you are assessing. Make your label as specific as you can. Since you are about to jump down the narrative rabbit hole, it's important to have a reference point to come back to so you don't get lost.

2. **Declare the purpose of your narrative examination.**

   Again, so you keep in mind why you are unpacking the content in question, articulate what your purpose and goals are for doing it. When examining such intangibles, it is very helpful to keep your mission in mind so you don't get lost along the way.

3. **Score each question** about the content by assigning a score in the far right column where 0 = not at all and 10 = completely. Keep in mind that the scores are not nearly as useful as the dialogue the exercise will provoke.

4. **Write about each question**

   For each item scored, develop a written response about the rationale for your score. If you are in a group setting, this will produce a wonderful dialogue and a description of the context, meaning and drive for the content in question. Consistent with your declared purpose for the narrative analysis, capture ideas for action based on insights that come up. In Narrative Scorecard Part 2, you will write out the actual narrative content, so this written work is about your evidence for scoring as you did.

Outcomes and Products:

If at the beginning of the exercise you are not sure whether you are dealing with a well-formed narrative or not, by the end you should be much closer. Second, what needs to be done next to make a strong narrative should come into focus as you work. Your action items will help you move forward from here to Narrative Scorecard Part 2 — the Qualitative Analysis. Part 2 will move you through the specific content of each of the questions you assess in Part 1.

Narrative Scorecard — Part I Quantitative

Name the content in question: _____

Purpose of this narrative examination: _____

DEFINITION		Score each line (0-10)
1.	**A narrative is an ecology of related, contextual stories that inform and define one's perspective.** Does the content in question fit this definition?	
2.	**Narratives emerge as a force among participants crafting perspective over time.** Does the content in question generate this outcome?	
	Subtotal (out of 20 possible):	

CONTEXT		Score each line (0-10)
3.	**Community**	
a	Narrators/Filters	Can we identify who initiated or actively filters this content?
b	Storytellers	Have multiple storytellers engaged with this content?
c	Audiences	Have identifiable Respondents engaged with this content?
4.	**Context**	
a	Era/Time Horizon	Is this content related to the current era?
b	Rate of Change	Is this content in sync with the rate of change affecting it?
c	Geography/Networks	Does this content sync with the geography/networks it addresses?
	Subtotal (out of 60 possible):	

MEANING		Score each line (0-10)
5.	**Current Meaning (Narrative in Background)**	
a	Current Assumptions	Can we identify current Respondent assumptions about this content?
b	Current Belief System	Can we describe current Respondent beliefs about this content?
c	Current Aspirations	Can we describe current Respondent aspirations about this content?
d	Current Linguistic Frames	Can we explain the current linguistic frames used with this content?
6.	**New Meaning (New Contrasting Narrative)**	
a	New Assumptions	Can we identify new Respondent assumptions from this new content?
b	New Belief System	Can we describe new Respondent beliefs based on this new content?
c	New Aspirations	Can we describe new Respondent aspirations from this new content?
d	New Linguistic Frames	Can we explain the new linguistic frames used in this new content?
	Subtotal (out of 80 possible):	

DRIVE		Score each line (0-10)
7.	**Intent of Initiator**	
a	Values	Can we articulate the values and priorities of the Initiator?
b	Mission & Vision	Can we articulate the mission and vision of the Initiator?
c	Strategic Themes	Can we articulate the strategic themes of the Initiator?
d	Intended Layering	Is the layering clear?
8.	**Impact in Respondents**	
a	Changes Made	Can we describe changes in Respondents based on this content?
b	Actions Taken	Can we describe actions taken by Respondents based on this content?
c	Value Created	Can the value created for Respondents by this content be described?
d	Other Evidence	Is there other evidence that this content has had an impact?
	Subtotal (out of 80 possible):	

Total score out of 240 points possible:

Narrative Scorecard — Part 2 Qualitative

Purpose:
This tool shifts your attention from how well you understand the parts of any given narrative to laying out the specific content for that narrative. It helps you:
1. Get very specific about the context, meaning, drive and participants of a given narrative.
2. Spell out the narratives from the perspective of a Respondent versus the Initiator.
3. Develop the content distinctions you need for the narratives you initiate.

Participants:
This exercise is the natural follow-on from the conversations you started in Narrative Scorecard Part 1. You can use this activity as an individual to deepen your understanding of a narrative. However, the dialogue of narrative content is better conducted as a group exercise. Once the content in question is assessed using the instructions for Part 1, a group can dive into writing out the narrative content itself. Remember, perceptions of narratives can be highly subjective. Do your best to drive for objective evidence for your assertions about narrative. That will help balance out the inherently subjective nature of the exercise and keep you from veering too far off the path.

Process:
1. **Use the naming and assessment of Part 1 as a framework**
   Using the same boundaries of what you are assessing from

Part 1 will help you stay focused. As you go through Part 2, you will be revisiting the same conversations as in Part 1, but this time you will be writing out the actual content. Feel free to return to Part 1 as you do, and change your scoring where understanding improves as you write out narrative content.

2. **Write about each question**

   For each item on the Part 2 scorecard, develop a full written response to the content for that item. Remember to go back to the Minimal Narrative Formula for your initial impressions of the narrative content. If you are in a group setting, this will produce a wonderful dialogue and a description of the context, meaning and drive for the content in question. Consistent with your declared purpose for the narrative analysis, capture ideas for action based on insights that come up.

3. **Revise the Minimal Narrative Formula**

   After you have completed the writing exercises of Part 2, build a revised Minimal Narrative Formula for your narrative. If you have done a good job of working the writing assignment, you'll have a fairly easy job of condensing it down to complete the eight sections of the Minimal Narrative Formula.

Outcomes and Products:

After completing Parts 1 and 2, you will have the context, meaning, and drive sorted for a well-formed narrative.

Narrative Scorecard — Part 2 Qualitative

Name the content in question: _____

Purpose of this narrative examination:_____

CONTEXT		
3.	**Community**	
a	Narrators/Filters	List the names of Initiators and/or active filters of this content
b	Storytellers	List the storytellers engaged with this content
c	Audiences	List the Respondents that engage with this content
4.	**Context**	
a	Era/Time Horizon	Choose a year range that reasonably bounds this narrative
b	Rate of Change	In what ways is this content in or out of sync with the rate of change?
c	Geography/Networks	Describe the geography and/or networks this content addresses

MEANING		
5.	**Current Meaning (Narrative in Background)**	
a	Current Assumptions	Write out the current Respondent assumptions about this content
b	Current Belief System	Articulate the current Respondent beliefs about this content
c	Current Aspirations	Describe current Respondent aspirations about this content
d	Current Linguistic Frames	List and explain the current linguistic frames used with this content
6.	**New Meaning (New Contrasting Narrative)**	
a	New Assumptions	Write out the new Respondent assumptions from the new narrative
b	New Belief System	Articulate the new Respondent beliefs from the new narrative
c	New Aspirations	Describe new Respondent aspirations from the new narrative
d	New Linguistic Frames	List and explain the new linguistic frames, what they enable and inhibit

DRIVE		
7.	**Intent of Initiator**	
a	Values	Articulate the values and priorities of the Initiator
b	Mission & Vision	Articulate the mission and vision of the Initiator
c	Strategic Themes	Articulate the strategic themes of the Initiator
d	Intended Layering	Describe the intended media layering
8.	**Impact in Respondents**	
a	Changes Made	Describe changes in Respondents based on the new narrative
b	Actions Taken	Describe actions taken by Respondents based on the new narrative
c	Value Created	Describe the value created for Respondents by the new narrative
d	Other Evidence	Write out other evidence that this content has had an impact

To take this to the next level, return to Chapter 6 — "Narrative Anatomy 101" — and develop content that matches the types outlined in the four sections there: Nomenclature and Frames, Resistance Honored, Inspiration Ignited and Stories Enabled.

To test your work, you'll want to revisit Chapter 5 for the Respondent-centric attributes that every narrative must possess: Authenticity, Relatable Connections and a Call to Action.

In the following section you'll find an outline for the Narrative Design Session Series. The steps outlined there will give you ideas for how to work a narrative at depth, from soup to nuts.

Narrative Design Session Series

Purpose

As mentioned previously, this tool will give you the outline for a series of Narrative Design Sessions. The tool set and process outlined here are for in-depth narrative assessment and initiation.

Participants

This level of detailed work is almost always a team effort. There are elements of this tool set and process that can be accomplished by individuals, but more likely than not, a team will be required for the best outcomes. 21st Century Narrative can conduct these sessions with members of your organization if you want facilitation and subject-matter expertise to round out your team.

Outcomes

When this scope of work is implemented from end to end, the outcome is a very powerful narrative, one that is well-crafted and understood by all contributing to its initiation. In 21st Century

Narrative Design Sessions, every element of the narrative-crafting process is worked in depth using accelerated learning and collaboration methods. These approaches ensure that all involved are aligned not only on the outcomes of narrative analysis and initiation, but aligned on the rationale leading up to them. The deliverables from this series are outlined in the following pages.

Process

Presenting the detailed flow of each Narrative Design Session is beyond the scope of this book, but the following will give you a sense of what is involved. Generally speaking, the steps below will guide you, if you wish to undertake this work on your own, through a flow for narrative-analysis steps and narrative initiation (or redirection as the case may be), then ongoing monitoring and cultivation. 21st Century Narrative always custom-designs such work according to client needs, so this outline is intended to be a good generic starting point.

Regarding time commitment needed for design sessions, it is possible to collapse this flow into a few days or conduct more detailed work sessions over a period of weeks. The number of educational modules on narrative, story, organizational change and field explorations to deepen understanding of incumbent narratives and Respondents are all variables not covered here, but would be considered in the programming of a comprehensive Narrative Design Session Series. The scope, scale and resources dedicated to the process by project leaders set the depth, pace and duration of the overall series.

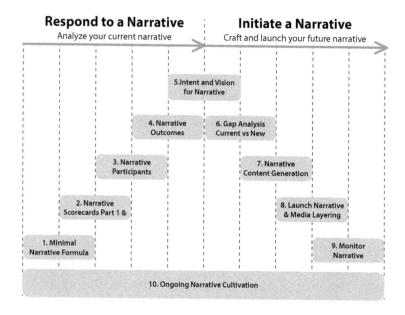

The Narrative Design Session Series would cover the following 10 modules roughly in this order:

1. **Minimal Narrative Formula** — A narrative description using the template is developed and iterated multiple times during this process until it is crisp, complete and well-tested. This becomes a living document that is revisited periodically as the narrative is initiated, launched and cultivated.

2. **Narrative Scorecard** — A scorecard is completed at the beginning with two types of assessment: numeric scores (quantitative) assessing the narrative's completeness and written (qualitative) responses to the questions specifically describing the current state of the narrative in question and what is needed to achieve full scores in every element. The scorecard is revisited several times during narrative building as a litmus test and guide for working toward

highest possible scores.

3.   **Narrative Participants Map** — A visual mapping of
narrative participants shows all participants (Initiators
and Respondents) and their relative levels of interest and
influence in relation to the narrative in question. This
visualization of participants gets updated periodically as
new Initiators, storytellers, audiences and other types of
Respondents come and go from the narrative landscape.
You can build the Narrative Participants Map by making
a 2-by-2 table. Make a 10-point scale along the horizontal
axis for influence over the narrative (0 = no influence,
10 = complete control). Make a 10-point scale along the
vertical axis for interest in the outcome of the narrative (0
= no interest; 10 = existential stake in narrative outcomes).
Initiators and Respondents are plotted on this grid relative
to each other. This mapping provides guidance on which
Respondents need to be complied with, which can be
negotiated with, which should be monitored and which
should be ignored.

4.   **Narrative Outcomes and Implications** — The first
part of this session includes an analysis of the outcomes
generated by the incumbent background narrative, and
then it projects the implications if those outcomes persist.
If the negative implications of letting the current narrative
play on are not moving enough, it's not worth the effort to
initiate a new narrative. If, on the other hand, letting the
incumbent narrative persist becomes increasingly costly,
this exercise will expose the importance of taking action
to change it. The second part of this session involves
building scenarios about a new narrative including its
expected implications and outcomes. This helps answer

the question "What's in it for me?" for both narrative Initiators and narrative Respondents. Likewise, both parts of this session assess whether the narrative in question is generative or regressive with regard to sustainability (environmental, social and economic) and human potential. If the narrative is regressive (destructive of sustainability and human potential), then changes should be called out to make it generative (supportive of sustainability and human potential). Depending on the scope and scale of the effort, this step may also include examinations of organizational mission, vision, values, strategy, organizational structure, culture, product and service offerings as well as other organizational attributes.

5. **Narrative Intent and Vision of Impact** — Based on the previous examinations, the Initiators articulate their vision of success with quantitative and qualitative elements. This step will include all elements of narrative drive as outlined. Again, depending on the scope and scale of the effort, organizational mission, vision, values, strategy, organizational structure, culture, product and service offerings, as well as other organizational attributes, may be included. The intention of the new narrative is articulated, including a vision for its impact among Respondents.

6. **Gap Analysis** — Combining the outcomes, implications and vision work, the next step is to describe the gap between current organizational state and incumbent narrative and a desired organizational state and new narrative. In the case of product or service narratives, the organizational elements and narrative may be deeply intertwined. In other situations, there may be somewhat fewer organizational elements to clarify. In any case, this

step articulates the distance to go from the present to the initiation and cultivation of the intended new narrative.

7. **Narrative Content Generation and Testing** — As we described in Chapters 1 and 2, developing narrative content has historically been the domain of advertising, communication, public relations and news agencies. But, as we outlined in Chapter 3, the Internet and the new journalism it enables put that role potentially into the hands of every narrative Initiator. In this step, using the Minimal Narrative Formula and the Narrative Scorecard as boundaries and guides, we can build out the Initiator's tools described in Chapter 6: nomenclature and frames, resistance and opposing voices, inspiration ignitors and stories. As content is generated for these narrative initiation tools, it is tested against what Respondents need as outlined in Chapter 5: authenticity, relatable connections and a call to action. This step is challenging, but if the previous steps are done thoroughly, and the narrative formula and scorecard are kept as metrics of progress, this step will move along until a vibrant narrative is developed.

8. **Launch and Layering** — Broadcasting the various manifestations of your narrative was also once primarily the role of advertising, communication, public relations and news agencies. For an organization, a new narrative launch could include the full array of agency techniques. For individuals, the practical choice of techniques is smaller. Whether you're a big agency or little startup, it takes tremendous focus and attention to detail to launch a new narrative well. In this step, we develop the initial programming and timelines. The narrative launch is planned, along with game plans for responding to

Respondents of all stripes. The layering of Respondent reactions onto a newly initiated narrative will begin immediately, including those of opposing voices. Planning to engage with all voices is essential, not just those that agree with the narrative's main messages. Initiators must have plans and resources allocated for engaging with Respondents as they question narrative authenticity, reveal what aspects of the narrative are relatable and demonstrate what calls to action get them off the couch.

9. **Narrative Monitoring** — Once the narrative is launched and layering is underway, the Initiator has a responsibility to the care and feeding of the new narrative. Using the Narrative Scorecard periodically, objective evidence of Respondent engagement can be monitored and tracked. For sophisticated narrative Initiators, there are search engine optimization (SEO) and data-mining (big data) opportunities to make Narrative Scorecard results very detailed and statistically valid. For less sophisticated Initiators, simpler tools such as social media counts (friends, likes, shares, followers, subscribers, etc.) are easy starting points. This step develops your strategy and process for monitoring the health and life cycle of your narrative.

10. **Ongoing Narrative Cultivation** — With the new narrative alive in the wild, the work of this step is to cultivate it so that the Initiator's intent and Respondents' impact are realized over time. Ongoing cultivation, using all the tools described above, will include generating and circulating new stories that further the narrative; sharing, liking and commenting upon Respondent stories and activity; and framing and reframing opposing voices so their messages

are utilized to best effect during the life of the narrative. As was mentioned in Chapter 6, "other background forces," including all manner of unforeseen or uncontrollable events, can, in a single day, create huge opportunities for a narrative or destroy it. Ongoing narrative cultivation certainly includes anticipating rapid change, preparing for it and then acting decisively when the moment comes.

Steps 1 through 7 outline a flow for a series of work sessions and topics that will analyze the incumbent narrative and then develop a new narrative. Following the guidance of steps 8 through 10, you'll be able to initiate, monitor and cultivate a new narrative to achieve the intentions and impacts you're after.

If this 10-step process raises more questions than it answers, that's OK. No primer on narrative would be complete without an FAQ (frequently asked questions) to help you think through some of the what-ifs.

FAQ

What if I've been tasked with developing a narrative at work but can't decide where to begin?

First of all, you're not alone! Until now, there hasn't been a tool for individuals and organizational leaders to understand, analyze and craft narratives. A great place to start, after reading this book, is with the Minimal Narrative Formula. Do the best you can to fill out each item in the template. Then have a conversation about it with some colleagues. Do this one-on-one at first, then as a group. As you do, use this book to help everyone develop a shared vocabulary about narrative. Half the battle is getting good definitions for these concepts, then working them with just a little bit of structure.

What if the narrative I am working on is so big that it's overwhelming?

There is some truth to the old saying "You can't boil the ocean." If you are facing a narrative project that is too big to boil, chances are some combination of four things has made the scope impractical: 1) the context you are working with is too broadly defined, 2) the target Respondents you are hoping to impact are too diverse, 3) the intent for the narrative is too ambitious or 4) your effort does not have resources commensurate with the level of ambition. Narrow the context, target Respondents and rein in the intention until you can work through the tools in this book with the resources you have. As you get a handle on a workable narrative scope and start generating results, you'll be able to attract more resources to expand the scope even further.

What if the narrative I'm working on seems to have loads of apparent Initiators?

Mapping the narrative participants (Initiators and Respondents) as outlined in step 3 above will help tremendously. Those Initiators and Respondents with high influence and little or no interest in the outcome must be complied with as if they are referees at a game. Those with high influence and high interest are participants you can negotiate with (whether that is in the public space or in private). Those with low influence and high interest (they have a great deal at stake) are at the mercy of the narrative for better or for worse. If they get aligned into a coherent group with a common message, they can become more influential, and may even become a force to be reckoned with. When groups coalesce around a shared narrative, they can change the course of history. Those that have low influence and low interest may contribute to the general noise in and around the narrative. They should be monitored for a changing position on the grid, but otherwise beware not to give them undue attention.

What if the Respondents are everyone?

This is a similar challenge to the topic of too many Initiators. To make your narrative-crafting task manageable, you'll need to apply discipline to categorizing and ranking Respondents. Using the tools outlined above, focus on those Respondents that have enough interest and influence to be meaningful to your intention.

What if the opposing voices are from sources I can't discredit, disrespect or disregard?

There are some situations where opposition to a narrative is coming from Respondents that have too much influence to be brushed off lightly. In such cases, all your narrative tools and skill may be required. Smart use of linguistic frames, traditions and cultural mores, and the various tools for inspiring Respondents to take action can provide the necessary counterbalance to oppressive opposition.

It is possible to offer a very strong alternate narrative that makes the apparently unassailable authority irrelevant rather than making it an enemy. Authorities, whether governmental or social, are only powerful if they are given power by others. If enough others are moved to act in a different direction without consulting that power base, anything is possible.

What if the stories associated with my company are out of date and making our narrative irrelevant?

The important related questions are these: What effect is that having on the company performance? And how is that impacting the mission and financial results? If you don't know the answer, or you know the impact is negligible, at least for now, then it will be useful to work with the narrative tools outlined here. Analyze what impact your current narrative is actually having. With those insights you can decide what new stories to create or what old chestnuts need to be reconceived to be more contextual, authentic and relatable.

While this is a common challenge for venerable organizations, there is some parallel to individuals, especially those in midlife or midcareer reinventions. If you're lucky, you'll realize that the tried and true worldview from your 30s will have a useful life and become outdated in your 40s — best to sort this out before becoming a 50-something midlife crisis! If you start an examination of your personal narrative, and really think through how it's working for you now, you can be proactive in transitioning to a new narrative for your next life chapter. As you do that examination, you'll ask, "At this stage in life, is my narrative still generative or has it become regressive?" The tools can help you think through how you are currently responding to your "traditional" way of being and develop some alternatives you might deliberately explore.

What if my company narrative is carefully defended by leadership, even though it inspires all the wrong things?

This circumstance is not uncommon, especially in organizations with strong executive leadership that is more autocratic than participatory. If you have this situation, a good place to start is to carefully and objectively analyze what impact the current narrative is having among your various Respondents. Second, quantify, if you can, how those impacts and behaviors turn into business performance and brand reputation. Without making a strong case, including the organizational pain, you'll have a hard time convincing leadership that, in fact, the wrong things are being inspired. From there, the question becomes: Who in your organization would be the most credible "opposing voice" for a new narrative, and can you influence them to participate? Once again, we're back to the value of mapping narrative participants, but this time they are internal to the organization, not external. Building an internal narrative with a generative call to action follows the same principles as building an external narrative.

What if our company narrative is actually regressive and we want to make it generative?

This is a very delicate topic. Whole industries have had to come to grips with the negative impacts that their product has on the environment and humanity. It's not hard to identify economic sectors facing narrative challenges in connection with climate change. Whole industries are dealing with this: fossil fuels, energy, agriculture (both animal- and plant-based) and forestry, to name a few. Halfhearted attempts to transform a regressive narrative into a generative narrative include concepts like "clean coal," British Petroleum's rebranding with a sunflower-like logo and the short-lived tagline "Beyond Petroleum." The tobacco industry has certainly gone through this process. The challenge is to be authentic in your narrative, not just to sound authentic. There are no easy answers to this very complex and provocative question.

What if our new narrative isn't landing like we hoped?

First and foremost, it is important to remember that most of the time narrative craft is more like gardening than masonry. A narrative is not simply installed — it is cultivated. Iterative cycles are an expected and natural part of narrative cultivation. That is one of the differences between stories and narrative. Stories are written once and delivered to the audience, while narratives are initiated and cultivated in a give-and-take with Respondents. If you think your narrative is not "landing," it's important to go back to the various specifics we've covered in the Minimal Narrative Formula and the

Narrative Scorecard. Use these for clarity about what you want from your narrative and how you will know if you are getting it. From there, use the tools to troubleshoot your narrative. Do the basic logics hold together in the Narrative Formula? Which of your scores are low on the Narrative Scorecard? Have you asked third-party observers or Respondents to help you with your assessments? If not, this is a great way to get feedback that is not concerned with only delivering good news to leadership.

What if I get partway through the process I've outlined and get lost?

You can use this book, particularly Chapter 7, to help with a process for narrative analysis and development. If at any point you feel like the process is taking you where you don't want to go, or if your circumstances force you to "go off-road," you can always go back to the Narrative Scorecard and ask yourself, Where is my narrative weak and what can I do to strengthen it? This is a nonlinear use of the tools that is always available to you if you have gotten lost or even if you have mastered all the processes and no longer need a recipe to develop and cultivate your narrative.

CHAPTER 8

CONCLUSION

AT THE OUTSET, WE declared that this book would help you in six ways:

- Understand what a narrative is and the dynamic conditions from which it emerges
- Recognize both the authentic and false narratives around you
- Become more conscious of the narratives in your life, organization and community so you can exert choice to align with or modify narratives to which you are a Respondent
- Appreciate the fundamental roles people play as Respondents and Initiators of narrative
- Understand the building blocks that make up a narrative
- Create new narratives for personal, business or community improvement

In Chapter 1, we offered a definition of narrative as a logical level above stories: A narrative is an ecology of related, contextual stories that inform and define one's perspective. We presented an explanation for the sense of information overload nearly everyone experiences, including that nagging feeling that we are being molded by narratives in the world around us, mostly without considering where they are taking us. Where are the narratives at work in your life taking you?

In Chapter 2, we explored more deeply the need for a unifying narrative. Applying a narrative to the stream of stories flying by helps us connect the various story lines to form a coherent image. If our narrative puts enough pieces into contrast against the rest, clear, contextualized and relevant meaning is the product. If it is clear enough, we can communicate a coherent vision and act upon it. We offered examples throughout the book of how some narratives get so strong that they prevent people from embracing facts that contradict the narrative. We asserted in the second half of our definition that narratives emerge as a force among participants crafting perspective over time. As a "force," narratives move people, and that in turn causes the movement of money, power, political will, business decisions and consumer behavior. Those who harness the force of narrative have power to improve themselves and the world. Those who are deliberate Initiators of narrative connect the dots in the chaos and gain authorship of the narratives they live by. Who initiated the narratives you live by?

In Chapter 3, we observed how a new form of journalism has made irrelevant the map that people and organizations used to navigate by for trusted information. In the past, public relations firms would get company stories out into the world. PR people had tools to create buzz for clients. Now the whole world is buzzing, so new stories get lost. Furthermore, things are much more complicated today. Not only is it hard for organizations to get their messages out, but for consumers it's even harder to get trusted information in. Reaching audiences is increasingly difficult for those working in media, business and social justice. Sorting fact from fiction (and the straight shooters from the bull shooters) is hard. Audiences are becoming increasingly sophisticated and see through fake "content," so it is really tough to make meaning without a narrative that helps us filter and synthesize.

In Chapter 4, we explored differences between narrative and storytelling. We also distinguished between narrative Initiators and Respondents and how they can exchange overlapping roles. Here and elsewhere in the book, we touched on how narrative counterpoints and alternative intentions are important components to appreciate and even leverage. Remember, however, that narrative Initiators have to relinquish control as their narrative takes on a life of its own. Steering the evolution of a narrative is largely a matter of resources, but even those with nearly unlimited energy to throw at a narrative can be subverted by the public when certain nerves are pinched or if their narrative is shown to be inauthentic.

In Chapter 5, we outlined the elements that Respondents require of a narrative: that it be authentic, relatable and have a call to action. When narrative Initiators make factually truthful claims that are credible and demonstrate a degree of vulnerability, they can earn credibility and trust from their Respondents. An audience that has been lied to can turn on Initiators with all the powers of new journalism. Respondents can elevate a narrative if it is authentic, or destroy it if they detect a lie. Assuming a narrative gets over the authenticity hurdle, it still must pass the test of relatability. To do so, it must be contextual — that is to say, relevant to the era, geography and/or network of the targeted Respondents. It must also connect to the values, principles and aspirations of the Respondents. If they can't relate to it, there will be little or no impact. Lastly, we covered how important it is for a narrative to have a clear call to action. Without inspiring a change in thinking, feeling, behavior and/or buying, the narrative won't have made a difference. If, on the other hand, a narrative is perceived as authentic, is relatable and has a compelling call to action, it can cause the world to change.

In Chapter 6, we dissected the anatomy of a narrative. Become conscious of the narratives you respond to and the ways you further narratives, intentionally or absentmindedly. Doing so is part of taking command of your personal and professional life. For organizations, it's a necessity for success.

We outlined how narrative Initiators frame, craft and deploy narrative, and how various tools get used to maintain and evolve those narratives. We described how special nomenclature and linguistic frames set up Respondent assumptions, and how special words and nomenclature can influence thinking, behavior and even personal identity. We also touched on how story structure can make narratives compelling or forgettable. We described how important it is to leverage opposing voices for contrast and, if possible, even frame that opposition so that it directs audience attention to help the narrative while leaving open degrees of freedom that help the Initiators achieve their intent.

In Chapter 6, we also showed that stories are a very powerful component of narrative and give it strength when they are valid and sincere, connecting and relatable, and have identifiable storytellers. Lastly, narrative craft always offers a call to action, a path to a positive vision or a problem solution.

In Chapter 7, we covered how to analyze, develop, initiate, monitor and cultivate narratives from three levels: 1) the Minimum Narrative Formula, 2) Narrative Scorecard — from quantitative and qualitative approaches and 3) Narrative Design Session Series. The time and resources you have for narrative craft will determine which of these tools you will employ. We also addressed 10 frequently asked questions to give you some ideas about how to handle challenges and issues with common narrative craft.

While we could not make an exhaustive study of narrative in this slim volume, it is our sincere hope that, from the seven chapters reviewed above, you've got what you need to explore, learn, analyze and initiate your own narratives.

Before we bring this book to a close, we want to revisit the business case for deliberately working with your narratives. Whether you are part of a multinational organization or an individual trying to get a handle on your career, we know this work can make a difference. So how do we think about the ROI (return on investment) for narrative?

In this book we offered many examples of the positive and negative effects of narrative for Initiators. In some cases the narrative was exposed as inauthentic and the Initiators are paying for that now. As an example in the category of negative return on investment, recall the get-rich narrative that was so successfully managed by the infamous Bernard Madoff — until, that is, it was exposed as a Ponzi scheme. Madoff is now behind bars. The return on investment for his narrative was incredibly high for Madoff, until the narrative fell apart.

So even if you have infinite resources, you can't maintain an inauthentic and regressive narrative forever. But even if you have very few resources, you can take aim at those regressive narratives and bring people into the light. Always remember: Authenticity, relatability and a call to action can move heaven and earth. Patagonia proved how business improves when you give people a path for doing the right thing.

In the marketing and advertising world, it's not always possible to measure narrative impact with traditional metrics. Some new approaches to track narrative efficacy include increased searches, social media shares and conversations about your narrative — especially where your narrative's nomenclature and special words are used. This is one way to "tag" your narrative. Where those words go, so goes your narrative, and in that respect you can track your narrative's movements. Measurement isn't always practical, but metrics can help you know if your call to action is working. The idea that you can't measure what you don't track applies to narratives as much as to any other aspect of organizational performance and business.

Lastly, persistence of your narrative is a good indicator that it has hit a chord with an audience. In addition, you can also look toward the number of individual narrators and "sharers" that your narrative has spawned as it grows and evolves in the public space.

There is nothing more satisfying than knowing you have initiated a narrative that has grown into a force for good, one that is circulating freely in the hearts, minds and hands of people all over the world. There is nothing more satisfying than knowing you are responding to narratives that are good for you.

About the Authors

Ann Badillo

Ann Badillo is a leading business strategist and advisor to executives, entrepreneurs and organizations. She is currently working in the intersection of narrative and ecosystem building toward systemic transformation in the 21st Century. She is exploring new ideas involving narrative, movements and culture.

Her professional life demonstrates a history of incubating and accelerating start-up ventures and ecosystems around the world. For the past two decades Ann's focus has been in designing large-scale processes and experiences to tap collective intelligence and sense making in order to assemble complexity and accelerate innovation across organizations. She is the inventor of the Book Swarm™ process that launched this book and the Narrative Project. Ann lives in Palo Alto with her husband and they have two young adult children who are finding their way in the world. She is a graduate of University of California, Davis where she studied earth science.

www.badillo.com
ann@21CenturyNarrative.com

Tim Donovan

Tim has more than 25 years experience in strategic communications and brand ideation. He has led teams at a variety of award-winning PR agencies (including Sparkpr where he is a Managing Director) and innovative B2B and B2C technology companies. Tim's work has been covered by high-profile news outlets like the *New York Times*, the *Wall Street Journal* and *Forbes*.

His diverse background includes work creating international marketing for public companies, founding of the first U13 social network and co-creating Conversational Whitespace with co-author Tobin Trevarthen. The breakthrough concept takes the best of design thinking and co-collaboration and mashes it together with the art of the possible to produce original first-to-market narratives.

Tim is native of upstate New York and a graduate of Ithaca College. He currently lives in Alameda, Calif., with his husband and their human-loving Amstaff Behr.

tim@21stCenturyNarrative.com

Tobin Trevarthen

Tobin is a leader in the traditional and digital media space where, over the last 30 years, he has pioneered new ideas and strategic marketing solutions that have generated over $1 billion in revenue. He had worked for and with many Fortune 100 companies as well as hundreds of Silicon Valley start-ups. Now entering his third act, Tobin is creating a "Blue Ocean" for the burgeoning always-on, connected world.

A visual person, Tobin founded Spatial Shift as a company focused on "rethinking next." It is modeled on the Idea Lab, the world of ideation, the re-discovery of Marshall McLuhan's The Medium is the Message and his drive to find fresh angles. He is also the co-creator, with co-author Tim Donovan, of Conversational White Space — a breakthrough concept that takes the best of design thinking and co-collaboration and mashes it together with the art of the possible to produce original first-to-market narratives.

He lives in the East Bay and has been married for 28 years to the best blind date he ever had. Tobin has a set of identical twin girls, a special needs adult son and a very empathic Weimaraner named Frieda. He is a proud Michigan State Spartan.

toby@21stCenturyNarrative.com

Joe Sterling – Co-Creator

Joe is the lead designer and facilitator of the Book Swarm event for The Narrative Project and a major contributor to the creation of this book. He is a founding partner of Rainforest Strategies, a consulting firm that leads, teaches and publishes on innovation sciences. At Rainforest, Joe is responsible for business-model development, product architecture, modular delivery packages and consulting methodology. He also contributes to the design of the annual Global Innovation Summit.

Joe has been a nationally-known facilitator and strategist for corporate, non-profit and government clients since 1991. His unique ability to synthesize complex dialogues into models and action plans has accelerated corporate innovation and strategic planning, community building and economic development.

Dorothy Pomerantz - Editor

Dorothy joined FitchInk as a managing editor in 2015. She got her start in journalism in 1996, covering local politics for a group of community newspapers around Boston including the Newton Tab and the Somerville Journal. In 2000 she joined Forbes' Los Angeles bureau as a reporter and, over the next 15 years, rose to become the bureau's chief.

Dorothy's Forbes work covered a wide variety of topics, from real estate to Hollywood, from the future of computer-generated actors to Kathy Ireland's billion-dollar brand. She ran the magazine's Celebrity 100 list and established her highly regarded blog about the business of entertainment.

Dorothy has a degree in political science from Vassar College and a master's from Northwestern University's Medill School of Journalism. She lives in Los Angeles with her husband and two children.

Alicia Bramlett - Illustrator

Alicia is a strategic graphic facilitator of MG Taylor ValueWeb, Cap Gemini Ernst & Young Accelerated Solution Environments and the World Economic Forum. She is currently practicing with The ValueWeb and serves global companies and executive leadership bringing to life vision, mission, and key initiatives.

(Endnotes)

i   John Hagel, *The Untapped Potential of Corporate Narratives*

ii Hagel, Business Innovation Factory talk, 2010

iii Vauhini Vara, *Why CVS Quit Smoking*, New Yorker, September 4, 2014

iv Nielsen, *The Total Audience Report*, Q4 2014

v   Gallup, *Most U.S. Smartphone Owners Check Phone At Least Hourly*, July 9, 2015

vi Daniel J. Levitin, *Why the Modern World Is Bad For Your Brain*, The Guardian, January 18, 2015

vii Leo Widrich, *The Science of Storytelling: What Listening To A Story Does To Our Brains*, buffersocial, November, 29, 2012

viii Michael Barthel, Elisa Shearer, Jeffrey Gottfried and Amy Mitchell, *The Evolving Role of News on Twitter and Facebook*, Pew Research Center, July 14, 2015

ix Bill Carter, *The F.B.I. Criticizes The News Media After Several Mistaken Reports of an Arrest*, The New York Times, April 17, 2013

x   Jon Ronson, *The Internet Shaming of Lindsey Stone*, The Guardian, February 21, 2015

xi Margaret Sullivan, *Did Reddit Boss Coverage Cross a Line?*, New York Times, July 18, 2015

xii George Lakoff, The All New Don't Think of an Elephant!, [Chelsea Green Publishing] Chapter 1

xiii Stephanie Friess, *Changing Landscape Places PR at Creative Process Core*, PR Week, January 21, 2011

xiv Peter Senge, The Fifth Discipline Fieldbook, [Crown Business] Chapter 6

xv Peterfrates.com

xvi ALS Association FAQ

xvii Jacob Davidson, *We Need To Do Better Than The Ice Bucket*

Challenge, Time, August 13, 2014

xviii   FDA Warning letter to POM Wonderful, February 23, 2010

xix   Andrew Zajac, *POM Wonderful Looses Bid to Block FTC Deceptive-Ad Claims*, BloombergBusiness, January 30, 2015

xx   Barry Petchesky, *The NFL's Response to Domestic Violence is Only Making Things Worse*, Deadspin, May, 7, 2015

xxi   Drake Baer, *How Patagonia's New CEO Is Increasing Profits While Trying To Save The World*, Fast Company, February 28, 2014

xxii   Lexus web site

xxiii   Brian Whitaker, *How a Man Setting Fire To Himself Sparked An Uprising In Tunisia*, The Guardian, December 28, 2010

xxiv   David Gianatasio, *Happy 25th Birtday To Nike's 'Just Do It,' The last Great Advertising Slogan*, AdWeek, July 2, 2013

xxv   Jeff Hopkins, *How Swagelok Fitting Helped Limit Damage After Japanese Quake*, Swagelok blog, February 16, 2013

xxvi   Steve Ells, *Comprehensive Food Safety Plan*, Chipotle website

xxvii   Arthur Anton, *The Value of Our Values*, Swagelok website

GRATITUDE

ANN

Deep bow to my husband, Stephen Pond for all of his support on this project and all my BIG ideas, and also for his love and patience. Additional bow to my daughter, Mia Pond, for her keen insights and participation on this project. I hope this book inspires my youngest daughter, Perri Elizabeth Pond to develop new narratives for environmental action and global climate change. I dedicate this book to my parents, Olly and Adolfo Badillo.

TIM

I will forever cherish this shared experience in co-creating an incredible body of work on a subject that is so close to my heart. I want to thank my colleagues Ann Badillo, Tobin Trevarthen, Joe Sterling, Dorothy Pomerantz, Meg Buzzi and Alica Bramlett for their tireless commitment in helping to bring this book to life.

I would also like to thank my husband, Brian Harrington and my mother Elizabeth Reynolds for their belief and support in this project. Lastly, I would like to dedicate this book to my father who passed this year. If there was anyone who knew the value of narrative to bring people together, it was Pop. Thanks Pop, this one's for you!

TOBIN

I want to extend a special thank you to my wife, Debra and my daughters Emma and Olivia who encouraged and supported me over the course this project. A special dedication goes out to my son Spencer, who continues to teach me about the value of a smile and to keep things in perspective when life gets in the way.

For emergent practices,
new insights and narratives

The field of narrative is still very much emerging. We invite you to visit www.thenarrativeproject.net to participate in our community and the book site: www.narrativegeneration.com for additional insights and sign ups. Follow Narrative Generation on twitter @narrativegen and Facebook Page: www.facebook.com/ narrativegeneration/

CPSIA information can be obtained
at www.ICGtesting.com
Printed in the USA
LVHW042039151219
640580LV00013B/739/P